JUNIOR ATLAS
OF **INDIGENOUS**
AUSTRALIA

JUNIOR ATLAS

OF INDIGENOUS AUSTRALIA

GENERAL EDITORS

Honorary Associate Professor Bill Arthur & Victoria Morgan

A collaborative publication of the Australian National University, the Australian Bureau of Statistics and Macquarie Dictionary

Published by Macquarie Dictionary Publishers, an imprint of Pan Macmillan Australia Pty Ltd
1 Market Street, Sydney, New South Wales, Australia 2000

A Cataloguing-in-Publication entry is available from the National Library of Australia

http://catalogue.nla.gov.au
ISBN 9781760984717

Publisher: Melissa Kemble
General editors: Bill Arthur, Victoria Morgan
Education and cultural consultant: Jasmine Seymour
Permissions coordinator: Benjamin Hewitt
Illustrator: Jenny Hale
Design: Natalie Bowra
Cover design: Natalie Bowra
Cover artwork: 'Kungkarrangkalpa Tjurkurpa', 2015 © Artists Aboriginal corporation / Copyright Agency, 2021.
    (See page 184)
Cartography: The ABS maps in this volume were prepared by the Geospatial Solutions Section
    of the Australian Bureau of Statistics.
Team leaders: Sally Clement, Kathryn Hooton
Cartographers: Jessica Newton, Jenelle Monahan, Jenny Lake
Map editor: Heather Crawford
Data tabulation: The 2016 Australian Bureau of Statistics (ABS) data in this volume were provided
    by the Centre of Excellence for Aboriginal and Torres Strait Islander Statistics at the ABS.
Team leader: Michael Bullot
Data analysts: Veronica Kerr, Sarah Chandler

Printed in Thailand

10 9 8 7 6 5 4 3 2

WARNING
It is customary in some Aboriginal communities not to mention the names of or reproduce images of the
recently deceased. Care and discretion should be exercised in using this book within Arnhem Land, central
Australia and the Kimberley.

Contents

vi

Introduction

An atlas is a book of maps. Information in a picture is usually easier to understand than a whole lot of words. Maps are like pictures, so they also make information easier to understand. The *Junior Atlas of Indigenous Australia* is made up of over 130 maps and over 165 photographs, artworks, illustrations and charts and graphs. To make the information in the Atlas more easily understood, each item is accompanied by a short piece of text.

The *Junior Atlas of Indigenous Australia* is a collaborative publication between the Australian National University, the Australian Bureau of Statistics and Macquarie Dictionary. It is based upon the two editions of the *Macquarie Atlas of Indigenous Australia*. The content has been adapted to suit a younger audience by the General Editors, Bill Arthur from the Centre for Aboriginal Economic Policy Research (CAEPR) at the Australian National University and Victoria Morgan, Managing Editor from Macquarie Dictionary Publishers. It includes contributions from more than 40 authors from a wide variety of places and professions – from universities, the arts world, Indigenous organisations and members of Community. Some additional material has been supplied by researchers and writers at Macquarie Dictionary, in some cases to update information, and in others to provide material relevant to the younger audience.

Jasmine Seymour provided valued educational and cultural advice to the General Editors. Jasmine is a Dharug woman and a descendant of Maria Lock, daughter of Yarramundi, the Boorooberongal Elder who met Governor Phillip on the banks of the Hawkesbury River in 1791. She is a primary school teacher, Dharug language teacher and activist, artist and a published author of children's books which integrate Dharug language throughout.

Teaching Notes to accompany this Atlas are available for download at panmacmillan.com.au

The Teaching Notes were prepared by Jasmine Seymour in conjunction with Macquarie Dictionary.

The Australian National University, the Australian Bureau of Statistics and Macquarie Dictionary acknowledges the Traditional Custodians of Country throughout Australia and their connections to lands, waters and communities. We pay our respect to Elders past and present and extend that respect to all Aboriginal and Torres Strait Islander peoples today. We honour more than sixty thousand years of storytelling, art and culture.

Exploring the Atlas

Maps

There are many types of maps. You may know of one kind from Google Maps or the GPS navigation in your car which can show you the way to get somewhere, like a bus stop or your holiday camp site. The maps in this Atlas are different from that – they show where features of Indigenous life were and are found across Australia.

Information in a picture is usually easier to understand than a whole lot of words. Maps are like pictures, so they also make information easier to understand. A map shows where things are in relation to other things. For example, a map might show if something only happens near the coast or if it also happens inland. But maps also have disadvantages. The information on them is often limited and quite general – they only show approximately where things are. To make the information in the Atlas more easily understood, the maps are accompanied by illustrations and short pieces of text.

Research of any subject is timeless – it is ongoing and never ends. The Atlas is based on research, some of which was carried out some time ago, and some which is very recent. However, none of it is the final story on the Indigenous world. Future editions of this Atlas and future research may very well update what you see here.

Types of maps in the Atlas

Indigenous forms of mapping

Traditional Indigenous mapping is a specialised subject which is explored in Chapter 3 Indigenous mapping of place and space.

Western forms of mapping

The majority of the maps in the Atlas follow the style of Western mapping, a tradition developed in Europe hundreds of years ago. Some features include:

- maps that show one or more features
- map keys that tell you what the features marked on the map are
- map titles
- maps positioned with north at the top

Each map is explained in a short section of text. In the text we often compare the location of one place with another place, for example, *Utopia is north-east of Alice Springs*. This is a standard way of describing locations using the position of the needle of a magnetic compass, which always points to the north. A compass has four main points called cardinal points – north (N), south (S), east (E) and west (W). It also has four other points located between them – north-east (NE), south-east (SE), south-west (SW) and north-west (NW). You can see from this picture of a compass that north is opposite south, and west is opposite east. When you are anywhere in the world and you don't have a compass, you can roughly tell where east is in the morning as the sun rises there, and where west is in the evening as the sun sets there.

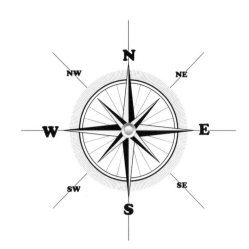

In this Atlas you will often come across these eight compass points when we are describing the location of places and items.

Australia's states and territories

We will sometimes refer to Australia's states and territories using the standard abbreviations for them (for example, the Australian Capital Territory or the ACT). There are six states and two territories and all are shown on this map with their capital cities, as well as on the detailed Locations map at the very beginning of the Atlas.

Most maps show all of mainland Australia and Tasmania, as well as some of its offshore islands, for example, those in the Torres Strait – between Australia and Papua New Guinea, or the Tiwi Islands off the Northern Territory. Several maps show the nearby coasts of Indonesia, Timor and Papua New Guinea. This is to remind us just how close these neighbours are, and in some cases, to help explain their historical impact on Indigenous people.

Many maps are accompanied by illustrations of the feature shown on the map, and these are explained in a short section of text. A small map is attached to some illustrations showing the general location of the item.

Bicornual split lawyer-cane basket
Tully, Qld

Scale

Most of the maps in this book show the whole continent of Australia. While you can see the whole of Australia on a map, it would take a number of days to drive from one side of the country to the other. Maps are produced using a scale so that huge areas can be accurately reduced to something that can fit on a page of a book. This allows you to easily see how certain types of information relate to particular areas and not to others.

The photos and drawings in this book are also smaller than they would be in real life. In cases where it is hard to imagine the real size of an item, a scale is given. Each division on the scale represents a number of centimetres. The scale will sit underneath or beside the image.

Two stone macroblades

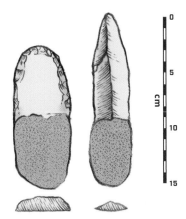

In this example you can see by looking at the scale that although the illustration is quite small, the macroblades are by far the biggest of all of the stone tools.

Thematic maps

Thematic maps indicate where features were or are found across the country. Features are shown as shaded or lined areas, or as coloured symbols. Thematic maps are used throughout the Atlas.

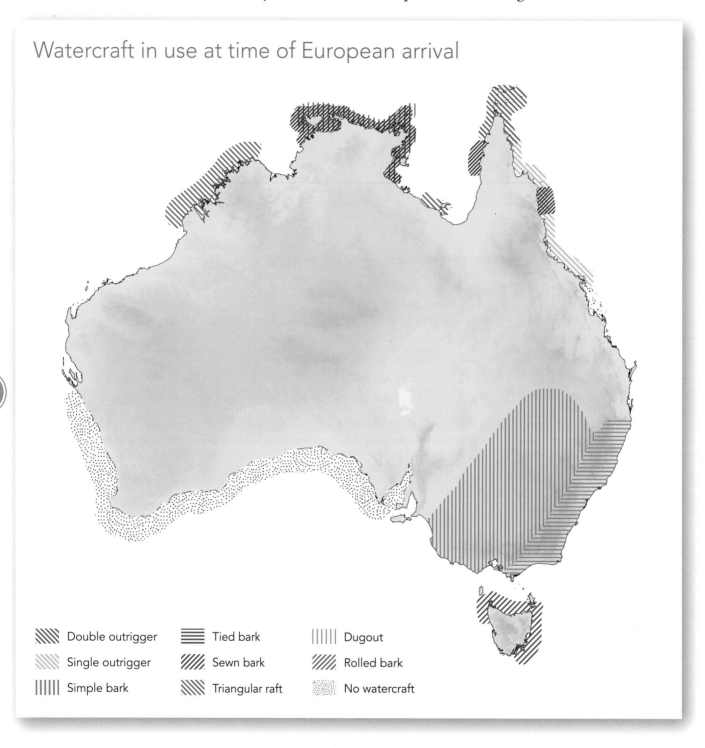

Watercraft in use at time of European arrival

Double outrigger	Tied bark	Dugout
Single outrigger	Sewn bark	Rolled bark
Simple bark	Triangular raft	No watercraft

In this example from Chapter 6, shading is used to show where different kinds of watercraft were used in the past. In the chapter, the map is accompanied by illustrations and text which give information on the different types of craft.

Choropleth maps

Choropleth maps are used to show the distribution of social, economic and statistical information. In this type of map, the country is divided into regions which are shaded to indicate values which are often given as percentages.

The data for many of these maps in the Atlas come from the 2016 national Census of Population and Housing. National censuses are carried out every five years by the Australian Bureau of Statistics (ABS) who aim to count every person in the country. In the Census, people can say if they are Indigenous or not.

People aged 15 and over attending university and other tertiary institutions, 2016

- Most 4.8 – 9.6%
- More 2.6 – 4.7%
- Less 1.2 – 2.5%
- Least 0.0 – 1.1%

Note how the map keys are labelled Most , More ■, Less ■, and Least □, and the values are shown beside them.

People aged 13 and over who identified with a clan, language or tribal group, 2014–2015

- Most 78.8 – 92.4%
- More 63.1 – 78.7%
- Less 34.5 – 63.0%
- Least 31.9 – 34.4%
-  Interpret with care

Some choropleth maps in the Atlas, such as this one, have been produced using information from the National Aboriginal and Torres Strait Islander Social Survey (NATSISS). The NATSISS asks Indigenous people questions about some social aspects of their lives. Note how, in this example, some areas are lined and the key says 'Interpret with care' ⁒⁒. This is because the NATSISS is a survey of a limited number of people and so in some areas it may not find many people. When this happens, map keys will say 'Interpret with care' to warn us that the information is not perfect.

Dot maps

Dot maps are used to show the location and size of a feature. Usually this is done by arranging the features into groups of a certain size. This type of map is also often used to show the distribution of populations.

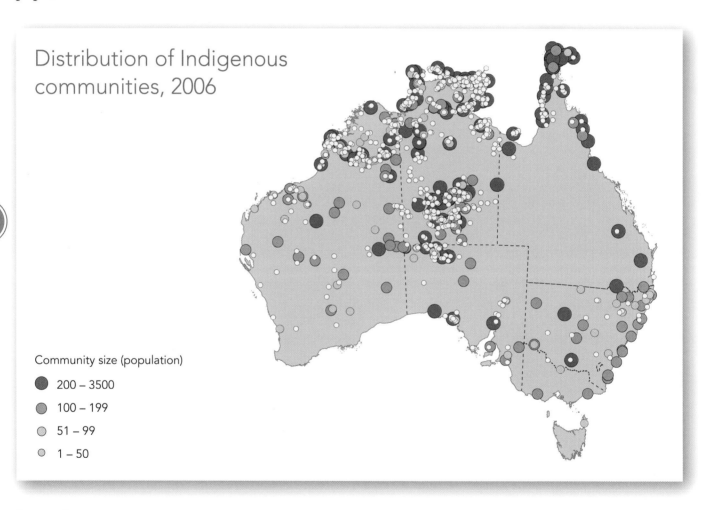

Distribution of Indigenous communities, 2006

Community size (population)

- 200 – 3500
- 100 – 199
- 51 – 99
- 1 – 50

Locations map

A map showing Australia's states and territories, capital cities and the places and regions mentioned in the Atlas can be found at the very front of the book. This map is the most detailed map in the Atlas and is extremely important as you can see where each location sits in relation to other places.

Timeline – Environment and deep history from 70 000 years ago to 1788

A timeline of important events from 70 000 years ago to 1788 and the beginning of the colonial occupation of the continent can be found at the very end of the Atlas.

Some special terms used in the Atlas

- The focus of the Atlas is Indigenous people. When the word 'people' is used we mean Indigenous Australians.
- The term 'Indigenous' means the people, their ancestors and their descendants, who were on the continent in 1788 when non-Indigenous people established an official presence. It includes Aboriginal people and Torres Strait Islander people.
- Where sections apply to just Aboriginal people or to just Torres Strait Islander people, they are mentioned separately.
- For other Australians we speak of 'non-Indigenous people' or the 'non-Indigenous population'.
- The term 'pre-contact' refers to the time before there was any actual contact with non-Indigenous people, and this varied over the continent. For instance, some northern groups experienced contact with the Macassans and sea explorers long before 1788. On the other hand, some others in remote desert regions did not experience contact with non-Indigenous people until 1984.
- The term 'pre-colonial' refers to the period before colonisation began in 1788.
- We use the term 'colonists' rather than 'invaders' and 'invasion' although colonisation can be seen as a particular form of invasion.
- The word 'Country' with a capital C describes the traditional lands, waters and seas of Indigenous people.

Helpful tips

In the Atlas you will see three types of pop-up information on the pages.

- WORD ALERT
- FAST FACT
- HOW DO YOU SAY IT?

WORD ALERT explains the meaning of words that you may be unfamiliar with. The word being explained in the WORD ALERT is also highlighted yellow in the general text. For example, 'are set in grips of resin and were made around 1890'.

WORD ALERT

resin

Resin is a sap produced by some plants, which can be used as a form of glue and in medicines and varnishes.

FAST FACT provides small pieces of extra, interesting information.

FAST FACT

Woomera is another name for a spearthrower. It comes from Dharug, a language of New South Wales.

HOW DO YOU SAY IT? shows you how to pronounce words you may not be familiar with. Each word that is given a pronunciation is also marked in red in the general text. For example, 'trialled in Ernabella and **Yuendumu** in the late 1980s'. You will find a guide to the letters used to stand for different sounds on page 159.

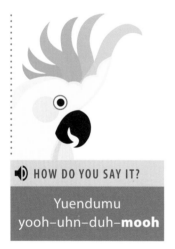

🔊 HOW DO YOU SAY IT?

Yuendumu
yooh–uhn–duh–**mooh**

The information in these pop-ups has been provided from the resources of Macquarie Dictionary.

Deep history

This chapter focuses on the first peopling of Australia, and on the technical changes they made over time to adjust to an ever-changing environment. Deep history is a term used to describe the vast expanse of time before colonisation. A great amount can be told from archaeological and geological research as well as from historical oral stories.

🔊 HOW DO YOU SAY IT?

Pleistocene
pluy–stuh–seen
Holocene
hol–uh–seen

The Pleistocene and Holocene geological periods

Geological period	Started	Ended	Main features
Pleistocene	Around 2.5 million years ago	Around 11 700 years ago	The most recent Ice Ages were in the Pleistocene. During each Ice Age sea levels dropped and distances between islands were shorter.
Holocene	Around 11 700 years ago, and after the Pleistocene	Ongoing – the period we are presently living in	The world became warmer, ice began to melt and sea levels rose. Around 8000 and 6000 years ago sea levels rose further and coastlines became more or less the same as today.

The Pleistocene is the name used to describe the geological time that lasted from about 2.5 million to 11 700 years ago, and is when the world experienced its most recent Ice Ages. The geological period that came after the Pleistocene – and which we are all presently living in – is called the Holocene.

In Australia it is common to talk about the places or archaeological sites where people lived and hunted as being in either of these two periods, and when possible, to give the actual date when they lived there.

The first arrivals

Recent archaeological evidence from east Arnhem Land in the Northern Territory suggests that Indigenous people first settled in Australia from Asia around 65 000 years ago during the Pleistocene period.

FAST FACT

Tasmania became separated from the mainland around 11 000 years ago. New Guinea was separated from mainland Australia, and Torres Strait and the Gulf of Carpentaria were created around 8000 years ago.

Bamboo raft

This photo shows a raft that was built by researchers using stone artefacts. The researchers were trying to work out what kind of raft would have been needed to cross a large distance of open ocean. The raft would have needed to be of a considerable size and sturdy. It likely had sails and steering oars to overcome strong currents.

Possible migration routes

Our planet has experienced several Ice Ages. During these cold periods, water that is usually in the seas and elsewhere becomes ice and the sea levels drop. When the sea levels drop, islands are closer to each other and sea crossings are shorter.

This map shows the coastlines of Asia and Australia at around 65 000 years ago when sea levels were around 65 metres lower than today. At that time Australia was joined to what is now Papua New Guinea and Tasmania was joined to the mainland. This is when we believe that people may have first come to Australia.

The arrows show the routes that people may have taken using some sort of craft to migrate between the Indonesian islands and Australia. This would have been the earliest sea crossing between continents by humans in the world.

— Possible routes

● Pleistocene archaeological sites

Landmass at 50 m below present

Australian megafauna

Megafauna were large animals that became extinct after humans arrived. Some researchers believe that changes in climate and environment were a cause for them to become extinct. Others see hunting or human changes to the landscape as a cause. This illustration shows an adult male with the animals to give you an idea of their size.

Pleistocene sites, 2014

Archaeologists have found evidence of people living and hunting over the continent during the time from when they first arrived 65 000 years ago until the end of the Pleistocene – around 11 700 years ago.

This map shows several clusters of places. This distribution may be connected to the quality of the environment and the size of the Indigenous population in those areas. However, it may also be because archaeologists have searched more for sites in these parts of the country.

Remains that have been found or dated from archaeological sites include:

- soil erosion in rock shelters
- rock art
- stone tools
- animal bones and teeth
- remains of plants, seeds and pollen
- human remains

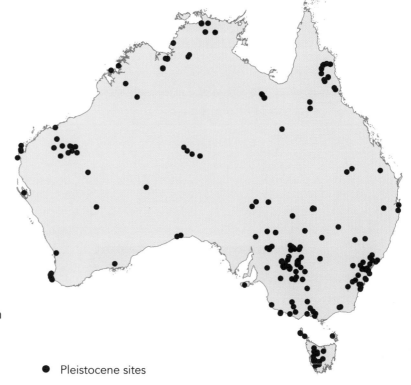

● Pleistocene sites

Sometimes the only evidence left of human presence in an area are stone tools. Wooden implements such as boomerangs, digging sticks, spearthrowers and shields are rarely found in these older sites since they break down over time. However, traces of remains have been found on the stone tools themselves. Studies of these have shown that stone tools were used for processing many different plants, animals, wood and fibre materials.

Two stone axe heads

The illustration on the left is of an axe head from Papua New Guinea. It is about 26 000 years old and about 15 cm long. It has small notches at the side to attach a handle. The smaller illustration on the right is of an axe head from Arnhem Land. It is about 20 000 years old. A groove has been ground into it to attach a handle.

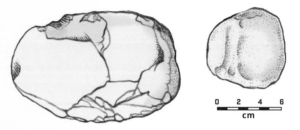

Two horse-hoof cores

Cores are one of the earliest stone tool types. They are pieces of stone from which flakes have been removed to make smaller and finer tools.

The two illustrated here are called horse-hoof cores because they are shaped like the hoof of a horse. In each illustration, the view on the top is looking from the top of the core and the view on the bottom is from the side. This is one way archaeologists draw stone tools. These examples are from south-eastern Australia but they have been found in similar forms all over the continent. No-one is exactly sure what their function was but it is possible that:

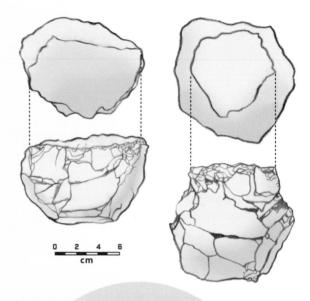

- the core was a tool in its own right
- the core was what was left after flakes had been removed to be used as cutting tools
- both of the above

ochre

Ochre is a natural earth pigment, ranging in colour from pale yellow to red. Ochre had many uses, including decorating a person's body and wooden items.

FAST FACT

Grinding stones are another form of stone tool found in the drier parts of the country. They were often used for grinding wild grass seeds to make a form of flour that was mixed with water and cooked in the coals of a camp fire.

Australia is also the site of the oldest human burials with evidence of ritual practices in the world. Found at Lake Mungo in western New South Wales, they are known as Mungo Lady and Mungo Man. They have been dated to 42 000 years ago.

Mungo Lady was the world's oldest known human cremation. Mungo Man was placed in a shallow grave and sprinkled with red ochre before the grave was filled. This is the oldest known burial involving the placement of ochre in a grave.

The Holocene

The sea level during the late Pleistocene and early Holocene changed greatly. It was only around 6000 years ago that coastlines became more or less the same as today. As the ice melted and waters rose it is estimated the coast moved by 13 to 24 metres per year in many places. In parts of the Kimberley it moved by as much as 130 metres per year. This meant that the people who lived in these places had to move inland and to higher ground.

Holocene sites

Archaeologists have found evidence for many more sites during the Holocene period, from around 11 700 years ago until the present. It could be that the population may have increased during that time but it could also be that more archaeologists have looked for sites in recent times. The map shows many sites along the coasts. Some of these are 'shell middens' which are the remains of shellfish that people had collected and eaten. Shell middens are very easy to see and you should look out for them when you are near the beach.

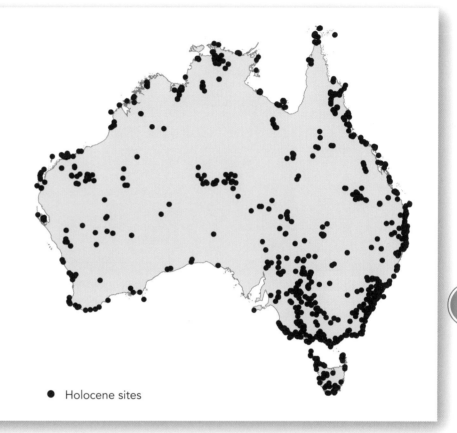

● Holocene sites

The Holocene saw new forms of stone tools developed for hunting as well as new ways of using other materials. Here we will show four types of stone tools from the Holocene period. They are followed by maps which show the distribution of each type of tool across the continent.

Two stone tula flakes

Tula flakes were used as woodworking tools. They were often attached to a handle by using the gum of the spinifex plant. The illustration on the right shows an example of this. A cross-section of a second flake is shown on the left. Tula flakes were found in a wide area across the hot and dry centre of the continent.

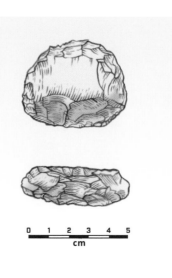

0 1 2 3 4 5
cm

Two kinds of stone points for spear tips

These kinds of stone points were mainly used as spear tips. The illustration on the left shows a point which is only shaped on one side – the back is flat. The illustration on the right shows a point which is shaped on both sides – the front and back. Stone points of this kind were mainly found in the central north and south of the continent.

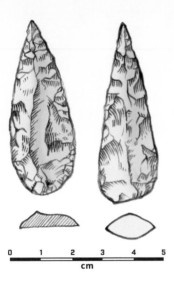

Two stone microliths

Microliths were small stone tools which were attached in rows to create the barbs of a spear. They were small compared to other tools. These examples are only about 3 cm long. Microliths were most common in the southern half of the continent.

FAST FACT

Microliths are also called 'backed blades'. They were not introduced from overseas but are the invention of local Indigenous peoples.

Two stone macroblades

Macroblades were very large tools and could be anywhere from 5 to 30 cm long. The two examples shown here, which are 13 and 15 cm long, are set in grips of resin and were made around 1890. Macroblades were most common in the north-west of the continent.

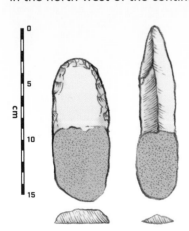

Kimberley point

The Kimberley point is a special kind of spear point. They were often made from glass or ceramic which shows how people were innovative by using materials introduced by the colonists. The points became highly valued by museums and collectors. This Kimberley point is 6 cm long.

resin

Resin is a sap produced by some plants, which can be used as a form of glue and in medicines and varnishes.

colonist

A colonist was one of the people who came to start settlements, called colonies, for the British government.

Distribution of stone tool types from the Holocene

These maps show the distribution of the four stone tool types illustrated on the previous pages: Tula flakes, Stone points for spear tips, Microliths and Macroblades.

 Tula flakes

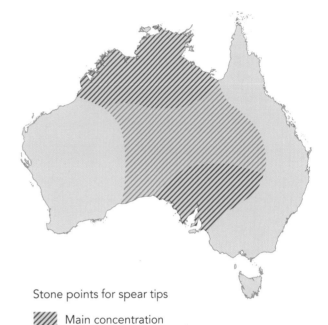

Stone points for spear tips

 Main concentration

Less dense concentration

Microliths

Main concentration

Less dense concentration

Macroblades

Main concentration

Less dense concentration

Hoe with shell blade
Torres Strait, around 1888

Shells were another material used for tools. This photo shows a hoe which was used to break up the soil of vegetable gardens in Torres Strait. It has a shell blade and wooden handle.

Arrival of the dingo

The dog was domesticated in South-East Asia around 15 000 years ago and was probably brought to Australia by people by boat some 3800 years ago. People used dingoes for hunting but also saw them as companions. A strong relationship developed between people and dingoes which exists in many areas today. It is possible that the dingo also spread from South-East Asia to other parts of the world as shown on the map.

FAST FACT

The arrival of the dingo led to the extinction of the Tasmanian tiger (the thylacine) and the Tasmanian devil on the mainland. These species survived in Tasmania because rising seas separated the island from the mainland and the dingo never reached there.

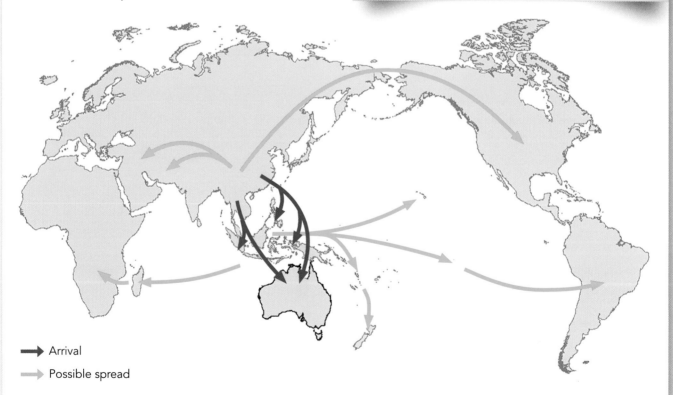

→ Arrival

→ Possible spread

CHAPTER 3

Indigenous mapping of space and place

Most atlases, including this one, are modelled on Western concepts of geography and the representation of space. They assume an understanding and use of mapping conventions such as compass points and scale. Indigenous ideas and representations of place and space are very different. They are based on detailed knowledge about, and connections to, particular places.

In traditional beliefs, the features of the land, sea and sky were formed through the actions of ancestral creator beings. Sometimes the beings themselves – or parts of them – were transformed into features of the landscape. These beings also created the world's animal and plant species, and gave birth to – or created – the first humans.

Torres Strait has its own set of mythical beings, separate from those of Aboriginal Australia, although they are linked to the creator beings of the far north of Cape York Peninsula. Their actions also led to the creation of sea creatures, plant life, geological features and the local people.

Origin and spread of the term 'Dreamtime'

The origin of the English term 'Dreamtime' can be traced back to the anthropologist Baldwin Spencer. He noted that the Arrernte people of central Australia use the word *altyerre* to mean both 'time of creation' and 'dream', so he thought up the term 'Dreamtime' as the English translation. The term 'Dreamtime' has spread from the centre and is now used across the country – by many Indigenous and non-Indigenous people – for the time of creation. 'Dreaming' has become a common term for the ancestral beings themselves. However, in most Indigenous languages, there is no connection between the word for 'dream' and the word for 'creation time', and some people object to the use of the term 'Dreamtime'. Torres Strait Islanders do not use the term.

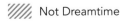 Altyerre

Dreamtime

Not Dreamtime

WORD ALERT

anthropologist

An anthropologist is someone who studies the beginnings and growth of humankind.

🔊 HOW DO YOU SAY IT?

Arrernte
ah–ruhn–duh

🔊 **HOW DO YOU SAY IT?**

Milingimbi
mil–ing–**gim**–buy

Walmajarri
wul–muh–jah–ree

Direction

Words for directions are often used in relation to the local environment. For example, the terms for 'east' and 'west' are often related to the word for the sun.

People are constantly aware of their own position in relation to their surroundings. English speakers often use the terms 'left' and 'right', using their own body as the point of reference – 'he's standing on my right'. Speakers of an Indigenous language will use a direction term as a point of reference instead – 'he's standing to the south of me'.

In many places, directions are used to refer to other people. The people of the ⟨Milingimbi⟩ area of Arnhem Land use the term *miwatj* meaning 'east' or 'easterner' for the groups that live to the east of them. A ⟨Walmajarri⟩ person in the Kimberley wishing to catch the attention of someone sitting to the west of them might call out '*karla!*' – west.

The distribution of one term for 'east'

The language terms for 'east' and 'west', which relate to the rising and setting sun are often used when giving directions. For example, the word for 'east' *kakarra* (or a related term) ▨ is quite common and is found in many languages over the centre and west of the continent.

▨ Where the word *kakarra* (or related term) is found

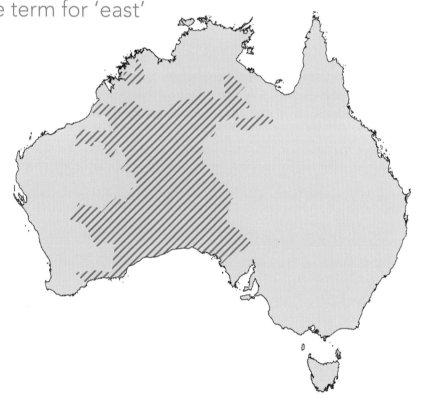

clan

A clan is a group of people who are related by descent from a common ancestor.

It is fairly common across the world to name a wind by the direction it is coming from. In both Torres Strait and coastal Arnhem Land, south-east and north-west are important because the year is broken into two major seasons by the winds from those directions. Winds or directions are often associated with particular groups in a local region.

18

Winds of Mer Torres Strait

On the island of Mer, each wind is identified with a particular clan grouping. People refer to themselves as 'south-east people', 'north-east people' and so on. The words all in capital letters are the names of winds. The capital letters in brackets are the directions from where the wind comes from. The other words in each division are the names of the clans they belong to.

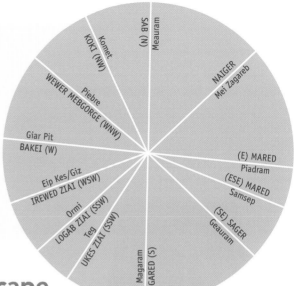

Representing the ancestral landscape

The journeys of the ancestral beings and the creation of the landscape were once celebrated all over the continent in the songs and dances of ceremonial performance, in stories, and in painted and sculpted forms. These forms of representation continue in many places and are the basis for much of the current art that is produced today for sale.

Although these painted and sculpted representations of Country can be compared to certain kinds of Western maps, the purpose for which they are made is usually quite different. They focus on the aspects of the landscape that are ancestrally significant rather than simply on geographical features.

🔊 **HOW DO YOU SAY IT?**

Guwak
goo–wuk

Marrngu
mur–ngoo

Malwiya
mul–wee-yu

Djarrakpi
ju–ruk-pi

Guwak (koel cuckoo), **Marrngu** (possum) and **Malwiya** (emu) at **Djarrakpi**
Artist: Narritjin Maymuru, 1974

This artwork shows Djarrakpi in north-east Arnhem Land through the story of the ancestral beings who created the landscape there. In this painting, 'north' is at the bottom and 'south' at the top.

In ancestral times, two koel cuckoos arrived from the north-west and landed in some cashew trees. Their travelling companions were ring-tailed possums and emus. While the koels ate, the possums spun their fur into lengths of string that became gullies to the north of the lagoon – shown as the stick-like forms touching the birds' bodies at the bottom of the painting. The ancestral beings then made more fur string that became the gravel bank on the inland side of the lagoon – represented by the body of the bird on the right.

Two women lived on the other side of the lagoon. After watching the koels and the possums, they made fur string that became the coastal dunes – the body of the bird on the left. Meanwhile, the emus dug for water but found only salt water. In frustration, they threw their spears into the sea, creating freshwater springs.

This painting can be read as a partial map of the place. The lagoon, and the gravel bank and the sand dunes are in the correct position relative to one another. But this map is not to scale, and it does not show every feature of the landscape.

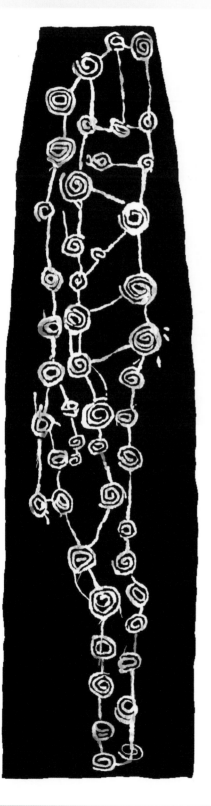

A map of Country on a Western Desert spearthrower

This illustration shows part of a design on a spearthrower. It was shown to an anthropologist by **Pintupi** people in 1957. The circular symbols represent the waterholes made by an ancestral snake during its journey through Pintupi Country. The names of the waterholes were memorised, and the spearthrower then acted as a map for the hunter who carried it.

🔊 HOW DO YOU SAY IT?

Pintupi
pind–uh–bee

The use of symbols

Both Western maps and Indigenous representations of Country use symbols to represent particular kinds of features. For example, in Western maps, water features, such as oceans, lakes and rivers, may be symbolised by the colour blue, and centres of population by dots that vary in size according to the size of their population. In Indigenous systems, symbols may be used to represent ancestral beings and their effects on the landscape.

Symbols used in Western Desert paintings

Unlike the standard symbols of Western maps, the symbols in the Indigenous system can have more than one meaning. The interpretation of any particular symbol depends on its relationship to the other symbols it sits with. It can only be 'read' by a person who knows the stories and geography of the Country being referred to.

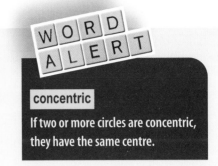
 rainbow, or cloud, or cliff, or sandhill

 this grouping usually means four women sitting

 two men sitting

 man

 waterhole waterhole running water

a spiralling line can mean water, a rainbow, a snake, lightning, a string, a cliff, or honey storage of the native bee

 rain

 concentric circles can usually mean a camp site, a stone, a well, a rock hole, a breast, fire, a hole, or fruit

 star

 footprints

clouds, boomerangs, windbreaks

 sitting-down place

fire, or smoke, or water, or blood

 travelling sign, with the concentric circles representing a resting place

---

Where toas were made

Toas were made only by the **Diyari** people from the Lake Eyre region of South Australia. Toas were small sculptures that represented particular places in their Country.

 Where toas were made

Toa Lake Gregory, SA, early 1900s

This toa is 40 centimetres tall and is made from wood, string and a soft white mineral called gypsum. It is painted with ochre. The markings represent an island in Lake Gregory where two ancestral women once searched for black swans' eggs. The two parts that extend from the top of the toa represent the two peninsulas of the island and the tips represent the colours of the stones found there. The painted circles represent the swans' nests.

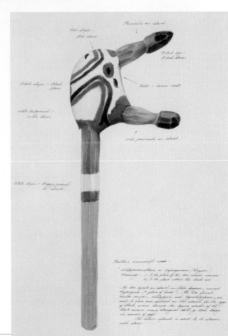

Modern Indigenous mapping

Traditionally, representations of Country were quite localised. They focused on the creator beings who gave form to the landscape and who link people to their Country. These kinds of representation are now often combined with Western mapping conventions. For some time, people have been involved in representing their Country in land claims and native title applications. They work with anthropologists to produce Western-style maps, but also use more traditional forms of representation. For information on land claims and native title, see Chapter 18.

Yawuru land values map, 2016

This map is an example of one new kind of mapping being carried out by Indigenous people for land management. It was produced as part of the Yawuru Cultural Management Plan following their successful native title judgement over Broome and the surrounding region. The map and its key show the distribution and seasonal use of a wide range of natural resources. It also refers to some ancestral events which are shown at the bottom of the map key. The Yawuru stress that the map shows the land and sea resources that they value, and it is one part of their plan to manage these. Other groups are also involved in this kind of mapping which, in other cases, is often called 'cultural mapping'.

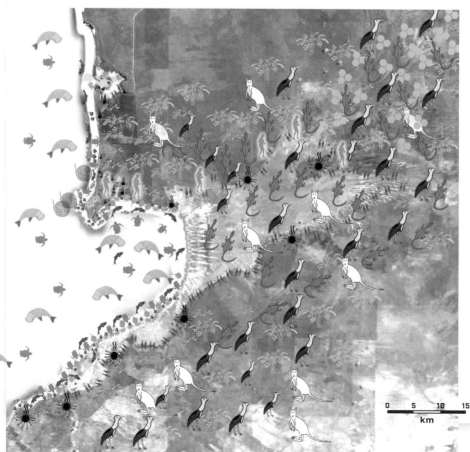

LEGEND

 cold-season fish: sand feeders e.g. blue-nose salmon/flounder/mullet/whiting/mulloway/dewfish

 nganarr (dugong) Barrgana [season]

 birndany (stingray and lemon shark) Laja [season]

 gurlibil (turtle), Laja to Man-gala [seasons]

 wanggaja (mud crab), soft shells in Laja time

 shellfish and coral, Laja time – before rain

 warm-season fish: reef feeders Laja to Man-gala

 warm-season fish: creek fish e.g. bream/grunter/mangrove jack Laja

 mirdimarlu (kangaroo), *barrjaniny* (wallaby) Barrgana to Wirlburu [seasons], 'good time to hunt as it is not too hot'

 jarlangardi (goanna) and all burrowing species, snakes etc. Man-gala to start of Barrgana

 girrbaju (bush honey) and nectar Barrgana, before rain comes

 barrgara (bush turkey)

 hot season *mayi* (bush foods) e.g. *gundurungu* (mangrove fruit)

 wet season *mayi* e.g. *magabala* (vine thickets)

 cold season *mayi* e.g. *yarrinyarri* (bush onion), *nawurlu* (blackberry)

 Bugarrigarra (Dreamtime) *jurru* (snake)

 wulgardiny (one-eyed snake)

 jila (water holes) and springs

 major camp site

 Bugarrigarra woman: a woman travels across the Broome peninsula spilling water from her water carrier, creating the water holes and soaks as she travels

 Bugarrigarra dogs: there is a story about the dogs who travel across the Broome peninsula from Reddell Beach to Minyirr

The Yawuru 'Knowing our Community' survey team
Broome, WA, 2011

This photo shows the survey team in front of their team bus, with the then federal Minister for Families, Housing, Community Services and Indigenous Affairs, Jenny Macklin in the centre. As part of the Yawuru Cultural Management Plan, the survey team undertook a series of major projects to document and build knowledge about community, Country and culture.

Yawuru seasons Broome, Western Australia

This artwork shows six seasons which form the basis of Yawuru people's understanding of what is happening on their Country – both on the land and in the sea. Their local knowledge allows them to read seasonal signs in the landscape that tell them where certain animals are, when they are mating, and when they are fat and ready to be eaten.

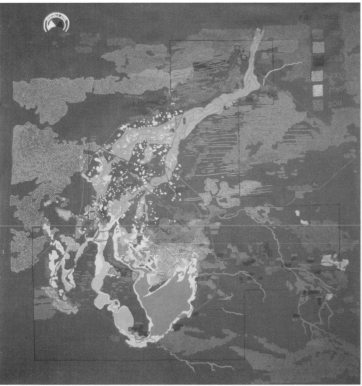

GPS for fire scar mapping, 2011

Indigenous people now adopt the newest Western technologies to produce maps for their own use.
In this example, the Traditional Owners of an Indigenous Protected Area, located south of Halls Creek between the Tanami and Great Sandy Deserts, used GPS (Global Positioning System) technology and satellite imagery to map the impact of wildfires on their Country. The map key is in the top right-hand corner. GPS technology is now quite widely used by Indigenous ranger groups as a land and sea management tool.

ARTWORK PRODUCED BY THE MELBOURNE PLANETARIUM AT SCIENCEWORKS, A CAMPUS OF MUSEUM VICTORIA.

CHAPTER 4

The stars

The southern sky is full of stories of the Dreaming. Indigenous peoples' careful observations of the stars of the southern night sky over the last 65 000 years have been recorded in their oral stories. Their knowledge of the daily and seasonal changes in the visibility, position and brightness of individual stars, constellations and star clusters is part of the epic stories of the ancestors who created the land and the night skies. Their footprints are the groups of stars, and also the dark spaces in the Milky Way. Indigenous people have used the stars to predict seasonal change, animal and plant behaviour, and to aid in navigation.

Star chart of the southern sky

This chart shows the stars and constellations in the Australian night sky. The constellations are in capital letters. Those marked in yellow are mentioned in this chapter.

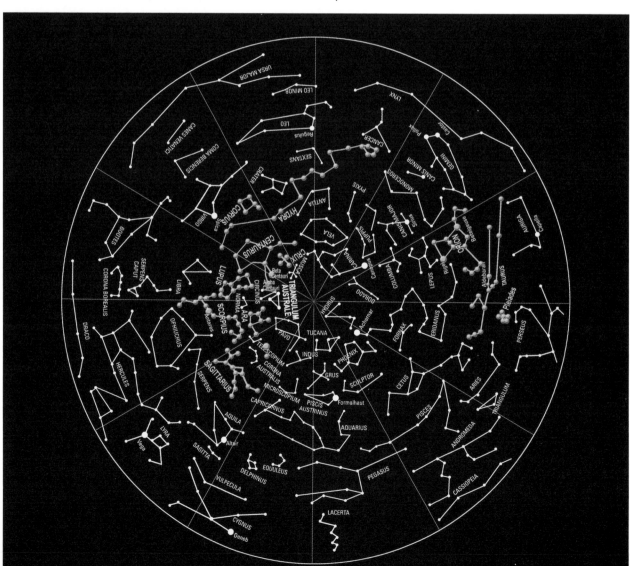

The Milky Way

A great range of the southern night sky is visible over a large part of the country. The land and sky are patterned with countless stories that show the connection between the stars and constellations with the land, animals, waters and seasons of the Earth below. Although people spoke many different languages, the creation stories of the Milky Way, the Pleiades and Orion are remarkably similar across the continent.

WORD ALERT

Pleiades

The Pleiades is a group of seven stars in the constellation Taurus. You say it **pluy**-uh-deez.

FAST FACT

In some parts of South Australia and the remote interior of the continent, the Milky Way is associated with fire. It is thought to be the sparks and the smoke from the camp fires of the mythical ancestors.

The Milky Way

Across much of the continent, people view the Milky Way as a river in the night sky. In Central Australia, it is believed that when people die their souls go to the dark place in the Milky Way near the Southern Cross – Crux.

REPRODUCED BY PERMISSION OF AKIRA FUJII/DAVID MALIN IMAGES

Milngiyawuy

Artist: Naminapu Maymuru White, 2001

The Yolngu people of north-east Arnhem Land call the Milky Way '*Milngiyawuy*', because they see it as a river in the sky that mirrors the actual Milngiyawuy River on their Country. They believe that when people who were conceived near the Milngiyawuy River die, their souls go up to the Milky Way. This painting represents the souls of these people.

🔊 **HOW DO YOU SAY IT?**

Milngiyawuy
muh-**ling**-yuh-woy

Yolngu
yool-ngooh

Stars and constellations

Some stars and constellations are associated with particular creation ancestors. The star cluster Pleiades is said to be a group of women – commonly called the Seven Sisters. They are being chased by Orion – male hunters. The Pleiades and Orion also signal seasonal change. The Pleiades (the Seven Sisters) are not seen in the sky during autumn and first appear on the eastern horizon just before dawn in winter. In the desert, they are known as the 'ice maidens' – those who bring frost. In spring with the warmer weather, Orion and the Pleiades are seen higher in the evening sky and they become clearly visible during the summer months.

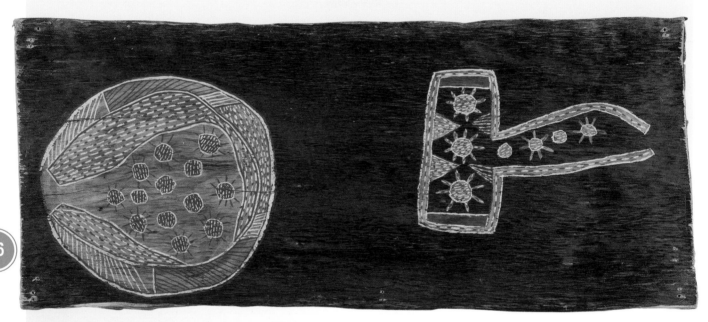

Orion and the Pleiades
Artist: Mini Mini Mamarika, 1948

The constellations of Pleiades and Orion are known by many groups across the continent as a group of women being pursued by a group of men. In this bark painting from Groote Eylandt, the Pleiades are the women represented by the shapes in the circle on the left. The women are being followed by their fishermen husbands shown as the three stars in the rectangle on the right. These three stars are also Orion's Belt. The fishermen are trailing their net containing some fish behind them, which are other stars in the Milky Way. The tradition of the Pleiades, Orion and the Milky Way connects the people to the sky and the waters on which they depend for a livelihood.

FAST FACT

Australia is in the Southern Hemisphere – the half of the world between the South Pole and the equator. The stars that we can see are different to those seen when you are in the Northern Hemisphere – the part of the world between the North Pole and the equator.

Seven Sisters Songline Map
Artist: Josephine Mick, 1994

This *Seven Sisters Songline Map* represents the connections between some of the Seven Sisters' creation journeys across Australia. It shows the Western Desert Seven Sisters' travels from Roebourne on the west coast, east through the Martu, Ngaatjatjarra and Luritja lands, then south past Uluru into the Pitjantjatjara and Yankunytjatjara lands. It then circles back west into the Ngaanyatjarra lands of Western Australia. The journeys are linked to Seven Sisters' sites at Narran Lake in Gamilaraay Country and with other sites in Bundjalung Country around Mount Warning on the east coast near the New South Wales/Queensland border. The Seven Sisters song cycles are sung in many different languages and this is represented by the large black circles with white dots around them.

CHAPTER 4

27

THE STARS

WORD ALERT

songline

A songline is a path an ancestral being makes across Country. It's often the subject of a series of songs called song cycles.

The stars of Tagai

In Torres Strait several constellations tell the story of their traditional hero Tagai, his canoe and his crew (figure a). In one version of the story, the crew consumed all of their food before they left on a journey. As a punishment, Tagai threw them into the water – sky – where they became Orion and the Pleiades – the crew. Tagai and his canoe are formed from parts of the following constellations:

- Corvus – his right hand holding a local fruit
- Crux – his left hand holding a spear
- Centaurus – his body
- Scorpius – the canoe
- Sagittarius – the anchor
- some stars in the constellations of Lupus, Hydra and Ara

The sketch (figure b), is a representation of Tagai and his canoe by a Torres Strait Islander.

Orion (crew)

Pleiades (crew)

Corvus (right hand)

Figure a

Crux (left hand)

Centaurus (body)

Scorpius (canoe)

Sagittarius (anchor)

The orientation of the stars of Tagai in the night sky was a guide to the various seasons for cultivating vegetable gardens. It was also a guide to the best weather conditions for trading voyages by canoe.

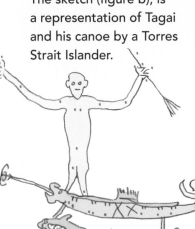

Figure b

HOW DO YOU SAY IT?

Ngaatjatjarra
ngah–juh–ju–ruh

Luritja
loo–rij–uh

Pitjantjatjara
pich–uhn–chuh–**chah**–ruh

Yankunytjatjara
yun–koon–juh–jah–ruh

Ngaanyatjarra
ngah–nyuh–**chah**–ruh

Gamilaraay
guh–**mil**–uh–roy

Bundjalung
bun–juh–lung

Hunting, fishing and fighting

Boomerangs, clubs and spears were once the most widespread weapons. Bows and arrows were only used for hunting in Torres Strait. Some weapons had special forms and uses and these varied greatly across the continent. Aboriginal Tasmanians were also lethal stone throwers, as the British colonists learned.

Boomerangs

The boomerang is one of the most iconic Indigenous objects. They are specially shaped throwing sticks used for hunting and fighting. They are also used for making music.

WORD ALERT

clapsticks

Clapsticks are short sticks of hard wood which are struck against each other to create a rhythm.

Types of boomerangs

The cross boomerang (a) comes from north Queensland.

Some boomerang styles are specialised hunting or fighting weapons. (b) is a fighting boomerang from north-west Australia. (e) is a hooked fighting boomerang from central Australia. (c) is a hunting boomerang from central Australia.

Others are more general purpose weapons, such as (f) from Cooper Creek in western Queensland. Type (d) is an example of a returning boomerang from south-east Australia. Although this is the type we usually think of as 'a boomerang', in traditional life people mostly used the non-returning kind.

Boomerangs

This map shows that boomerangs ▨ were used over most of the country. They were generally not used at all in Tasmania and over the north. The exception in the north was one area of the Northern Territory where they were used as clapsticks ▨ during ceremonies rather than for hunting or fighting.

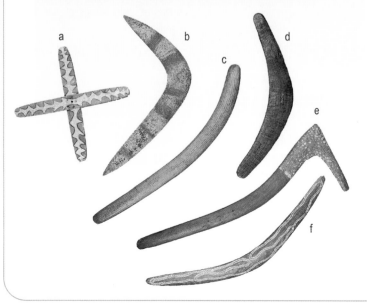

▨ Boomerangs

▨ Boomerangs used only as clapsticks

Use of the boomerang as a colonial icon

These four examples show how the boomerang has been taken and used as a colonial and modern Australian icon.

FAST FACT

The building plan of the New Parliament House in Canberra is based on the outline of two boomerangs!

Spears

Spears are used for hunting, fishing and fighting. They are also used in ceremonies. Some spears are made from a single piece of wood. Others are made with two or more parts that are stuck together with resin or wax, or tied together with some type of cord – these are called composite spears.

Single-piece spears and composite spears

Tasmania and some of southern Western Australia had only single-piece spears ▨ but these were also found over many parts of the continent. Composite spears ▨ were the most common type and were found over most of the continent. Composite spears with stone heads |||| were only found over the north, the centre and across the Kimberley. The map also shows that people used more than one type of spear in many areas.

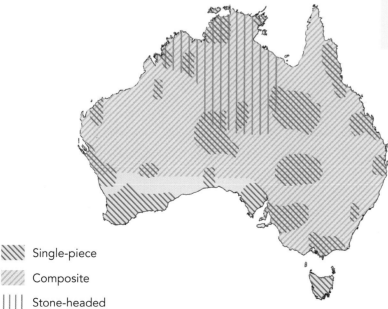

▨ Single-piece

▨ Composite

|||| Stone-headed

Single-piece spear and composite spear with stone head

This drawing shows two different types of spears. Spear (a) was found near the Pilbara and is made from a single piece of wood. Spear (b) was found in the Kimberley. It has a stone spearhead which is tied to a wooden shaft.

a

b

FAST FACT

Most spearheads are made from a hard type of wood. Spearheads made from stone often shatter when they hit something hard.

Multi-pronged spears

Some spears have heads with two or more prongs attached to the shaft. These spears are generally used for fishing. They are found mostly in the coastal areas of the north and south-east of the continent, and in Torres Strait.

An example of a multi-pronged spear is item (a) in the illustration.

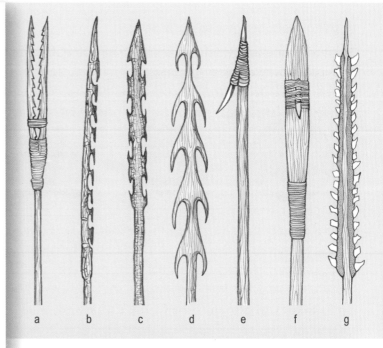

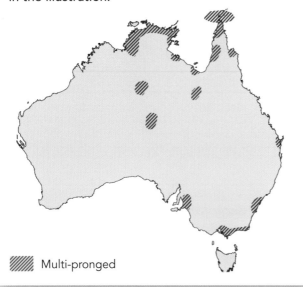

▨ Multi-pronged

barbs

A barb is a sharp point that sticks out backwards. Barbs are often used on the heads or the shafts of spears as well as on fish hooks to help hold or catch something.

WORD ALERT

Barbed spears

Spears with barbs cut into the wooden head of the shaft ▨ are found mostly in the north, west and south-east. They vary significantly in style across the continent. A style with detachable barbs ▨ are seen in the area stretching from the south of Western Australia all the way up and across to Torres Strait. Spears with barbs of small stone flakes on the head of the shaft ⦀ are less common. As with other types of spears, people used more than one type in many areas.

Examples of the types of spear in this map are items (b) to (g) in the illustration.

▨ Barbs cut into wood

▨ Detachable barbs

⦀ Stone flakes

Multi-pronged and barbed spears

The main material for making spears is wood, and this is the same for most traditional hunting tools and weapons. However, other materials such as bone, resin, sinew and stone were sometimes used.

(a) is a multi-pronged spear from Groote Eylandt, Northern Territory with two barbed prongs tied to the shaft. This type of spear is still often used for fishing.

(b) is a barbed spear from north Australia with the barbs cut into the shaft along just one edge.

(c) and (d) are barbed spears from Western Australia and Victoria with the barbs cut into both edges of the shaft.

(e) is a barbed spear from Queensland that has a detachable barb made of bone.

(f) is a barbed spear from central Australia with a wood barb and head that are joined with kangaroo sinew and resin.

(g) is a barbed spear from north Queensland with stone flakes attached to the head with resin.

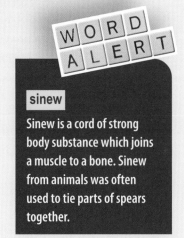

WORD ALERT

sinew

Sinew is a cord of strong body substance which joins a muscle to a bone. Sinew from animals was often used to tie parts of spears together.

Learning to spear fish
Arnhem Land, NT, 1991

This photo shows a young boy learning to spear fish. His spear has a shortened shaft but the prongs are full-size.

Spearthrowers

A spearthrower is a strong piece of wood which is used to help throw a spear further. The end of the spear fits on to the end of the spearthrower where there is usually a hook or peg to keep it in place. As well as greatly increasing the distance a spear can be thrown, it also increases the force given to the spear. This makes hunting and fishing much more effective. Spearthrowers are made mostly from wood but they can also include items of shell, cord, and gum from the spiny spinifex plant.

FAST FACT

Woomera is another name for a spearthrower. It comes from Dharug, a language of NSW.

Spearthrowers

The three main types of spearthrower are the broad type 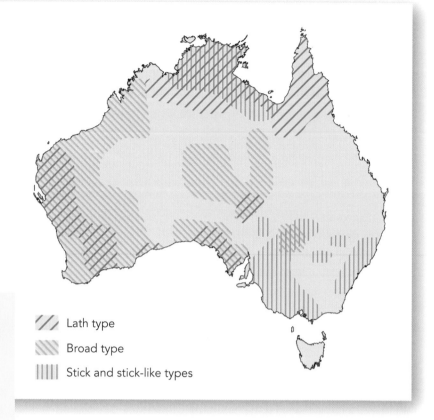, the lath type, and the stick type. The broad type is most common in the west and central parts of the continent. The narrower lath type is found mainly in the north and south-west. The stick and stick-like types are most common in the north and south-east. You can see on the map that people used more than one type in a number of areas.

Lath type

Broad type

Stick and stick-like types

Types of spearthrowers

Spearthrowers are often decorated, as in these examples. (a) is a broad type from the Western Desert and has a pattern cut into it. (b) is a stick-like type from the Roper River in the Northern Territory and has a painted design. (c) is a lath type from eastern Cape York Peninsula and has a shell handle.

a   b   c

Hunting with a spearthrower
Arnhem Land, NT

Spearthrowers are still used in some areas for fishing as well as hunting. This hunter is about to throw a multi-pronged spear using a lath-type spearthrower.

Torres Strait Islander weapons

The islands and reefs of Torres Strait lie between Australia and Papua New Guinea. While Torres Strait Islander culture shares a number of similarities with Aboriginal culture, there are also elements which are influenced by Papua New Guinea, as well as some which are unique to the islands.

While spears and spearthrowers were in common use in mainland Australia, bows and arrows were not. The Torres Strait is the only part of Australia to have used bows and arrows.

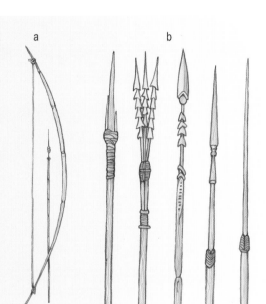

Torres Strait Islander weapons

The bows and their strings (a) were made from bamboo. Like spears, arrows (b) can also be composite and have many types. Clubs with stone heads (c) were used as well as wooden clubs (d). Harpoons were used to catch large fish and marine animals. Drawing (e) shows a wap. A wap is a barbed spearhead of a harpoon that detaches from the shaft to hunt dugongs.

a   b   c   d   e

dugong	A dugong is a plant-eating water mammal with front limbs like flippers.
communal	If something is communal, it is shared or used by several people, or it involves a number of people working together.

Nets and traps

Nets and various kinds of traps were used quite extensively for fishing and hunting. They took many different forms, including elaborate stone fish traps and specialised nets for taking both fish and land animals. Nets and traps are still used today in some places.

Aboriginal net hunting techniques were probably the most diverse and sophisticated in the world. Both men and women made and hunted with nets. A large net could contain nine or ten kilometres of handmade cord and take months of communal effort to construct.

Game nets

Nets ▨ for hunting animals such as kangaroos, emus and other creatures, and birds such as parrots, pigeons and waterfowl, were found over large parts of the east and west of the continent.

▨ Game nets

Ngarrindjeri **people driving ducks into a net**
Lower Murray River, SA

In large hunts of this kind, waterfowl might be driven for kilometres along a stream of water and hundreds netted at once. Once scared up off the water, the birds were kept on course by throwing boomerangs and other objects over their heads. They would think these were hawks or other birds of prey and dive low and fly along the water, until they flew into the net. People were allocated specific tasks to perform during the hunt, depending on their age and gender.

🔊 HOW DO YOU SAY IT?

Ngarrindjeri
nguh-**rin**-juh-ree

Remains of a stone fish trap Brewarrina, NSW

Permanent stone traps were used in areas where water levels in rivers rose and fell. The complex trap in this photo caught fish as the levels of the Darling River fell after rain.

Communal fish drive
East Arnhem Land, NT, 1936

The men in this photo are using hinged nets to scoop up the fish. In many parts of Arnhem Land, line fishing and spearfishing have now largely replaced the use of nets.

Fish hooks

Fish hooks of many different types were made from a wide variety of materials, such as pearl shell, oyster shell, turtle shell, coconut shell, bone, bird talons, thorns and wood.

Fish hooks

Fishing with several types of fish hook ▨▨▨ was common all down the east coast, around the south coast facing the Bass Strait, and in some of the shallower waters of the Northern Territory and Torres Strait. Hooks seem to have been unknown in Tasmania, across most of the inland and along the south and west coasts. Today line fishing with metal hooks is widespread.

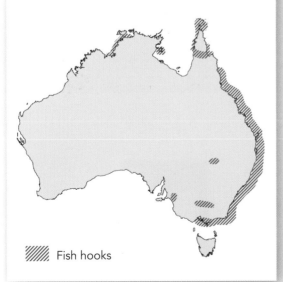

▨▨▨ Fish hooks

Types of fish hooks

The examples in (a) are crescent-shaped hooks made of shell from the Sydney area. Similar hooks are found along the central and southern coast of New South Wales.

The examples in (b) are turtle shell hooks from Torres Strait. These were probably made by bending the pointed end around a heated stone. This type was also used on the west coast of Cape York Peninsula in Queensland.

Types (c) and (d) are composite hooks from the Northern Territory. Type (c) has a wooden shaft and barb. Type (d) is made from bone.

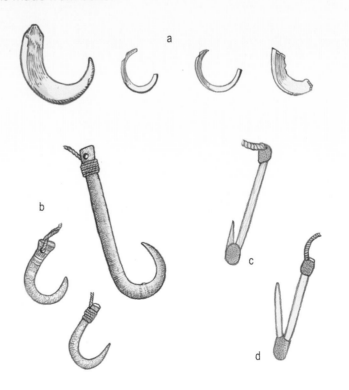

Regional resources

Food resources varied across the country, as did the methods and tools used for gathering and hunting. Some of the resources and regions not mentioned so far include the following:

- seals were hunted in Tasmania
- crocodiles, turtles and dugong were hunted in the north
- goannas, kangaroos, bush turkeys and emus were hunted over a large part of the country, along with other types of smaller animals
- carcasses of stranded whales along the coasts were made use of
- a wide variety of edible and medicinal plants and berries, and honey were gathered when they were available
- localised plant species were carefully tended and protected
- Torres Strait Islanders had gardens where they grew produce such as yam and taro

Some regional resources

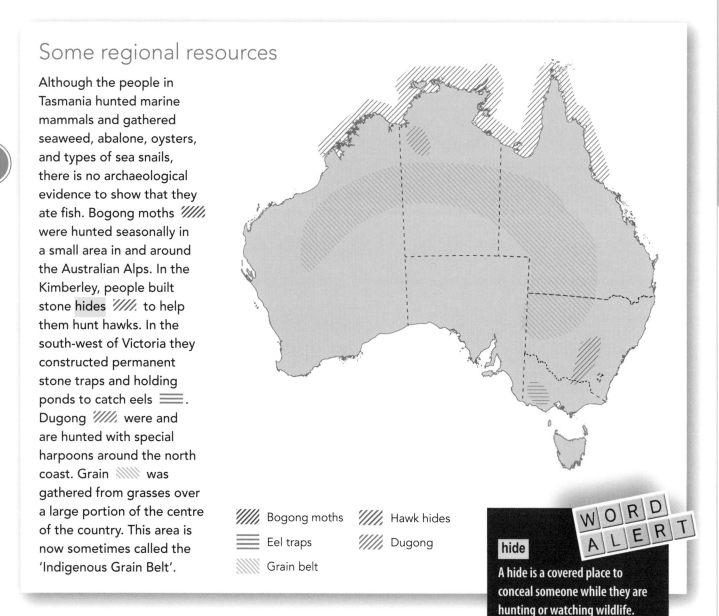

Although the people in Tasmania hunted marine mammals and gathered seaweed, abalone, oysters, and types of sea snails, there is no archaeological evidence to show that they ate fish. Bogong moths were hunted seasonally in a small area in and around the Australian Alps. In the Kimberley, people built stone hides to help them hunt hawks. In the south-west of Victoria they constructed permanent stone traps and holding ponds to catch eels. Dugong were and are hunted with special harpoons around the north coast. Grain was gathered from grasses over a large portion of the centre of the country. This area is now sometimes called the 'Indigenous Grain Belt'.

Legend:
- Bogong moths
- Eel traps
- Grain belt
- Hawk hides
- Dugong

WORD ALERT

hide
A hide is a covered place to conceal someone while they are hunting or watching wildlife.

Stone hide for hunting hawks Victoria River Downs, NT

Hawks fly in from different directions to hunt small animals during bushfires. This illustration shows a small horseshoe-shaped hide of stone which people in this region built to hunt the hawks from.

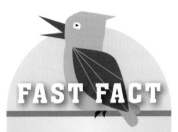

FAST FACT

Dugongs are also called 'sea cows'.

Platform for hunting dugongs
Torres Strait, around 1900

These platforms were used on moonlit nights for hunting dugong. The model dugong hanging underneath was to bring the hunter good luck. Today, small boats called dinghies are used instead of platforms to hunt from.

People moving to gather bogong moths

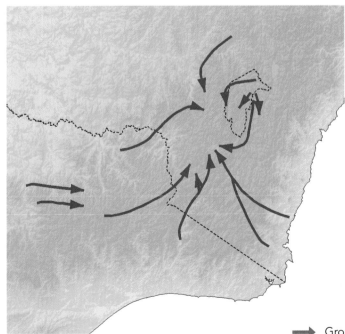

Bogong moths migrate to the Australian Alps from the west and north of New South Wales each spring. They gather in their thousands to sleep through the coming hot season on the undersides of the big granite boulders that are common there. Large groups of people from the entire surrounding region, including some from as far away as the east coast, would come to gather them.

→ Groups moving to Australian Alps to gather bogong moths

CHAPTER 6 Watercraft

Watercraft were used to travel from place to place by water and to fish and hunt. Because materials such as wood and fibre disintegrate over time, very little is known about the very earliest forms of watercraft. Dugout canoes and double outrigger canoes were introduced within the last few hundred years from Macassar and Papua New Guinea. Dugout canoes were made from hollowed-out tree trunks. Outrigger canoes had a float attached to one or both sides of the hull by long poles to give them more stability.

Other forms of craft such as bark canoes were unlikely to be the sort that brought the earliest Indigenous people to Australia as they were best suited for rivers and coastal waters.

WORD ALERT

Macassar

Macassar is a seaport of the island of Sulawesi in Indonesia. It is now known as Ujung Pandang.

Watercraft in use at the time of European arrival

This map shows that a large part of the southern and western coasts had no form of watercraft ░░ at the time of European arrival. The northern distribution of dugouts |||||| and outrigger canoes ░░ ░░ reflects their origins in Indonesia and Papua New Guinea. Sewn bark canoes ▨▨ are mostly found in Arnhem Land and Cape York Peninsula. Triangular rafts ▧▧ were mainly used along the north coast of Western Australia. Bark canoes |||||| ▭▭ were found over much of the inland waterways and coastal areas of Victoria and New South Wales. Rolled bark canoes and rafts ▨▨ were only found in Tasmania.

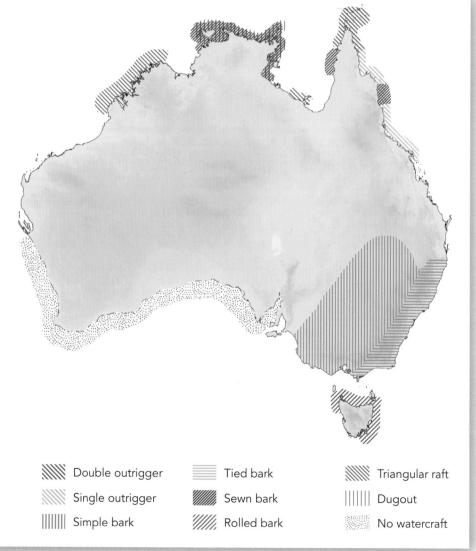

▨	Double outrigger	▭	Tied bark	▨	Triangular raft
▨	Single outrigger	▨	Sewn bark	||||||	Dugout
||||||	Simple bark	▨	Rolled bark	░░	No watercraft

Triangular raft
Glenelg River District, WA, around 1916

This shape of raft was unique to the north of Western Australia and the Wellesley Islands which sit off the north coast of Queensland. It was made from mangrove logs and could support several people.

Men in bark canoes
South of Port Macquarie, NSW, around 1905

This photo shows a fire being tended to in the middle of the canoe. People often carried fire in this way when moving from place to place by water. The fire was laid on a layer of sand or earth which helped to protect the canoe hull from the fire.

Dugout and outrigger canoes

Illustration (a) shows a dugout canoe. They were first introduced to Arnhem Land by trepangers from Macassar. They sometimes had a mast and sail which would have extended the distance they could cover to fish, hunt and travel.

When Europeans arrived, single outriggers (b) were in use in northern Queensland. Complex double outrigger canoes (c) were used in Torres Strait. These double outriggers were up to 20 metres long with sails made from plant material. Hulls for these canoes were often traded from Papua New Guinea as Torres Strait had no large trees.

trepangers

A trepang is a large sea slug with tentacles around its mouth. They are also called sea cucumbers and some people eat them as a delicacy. The people who catch them are called trepangers.

WORD ALERT

Goods were often exchanged by watercraft for use and as a way of keeping social and kinship links. In some cases trepangers from Macassar brought goods with them, and items from Papua New Guinea reached into Torres Strait and the mainland.

Exchange of goods throughout Torres Strait and with Papua New Guinea, 1904

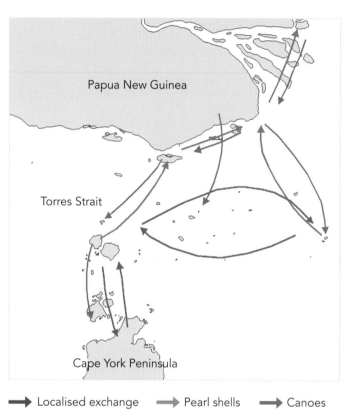

Papua New Guinea

Torres Strait

Cape York Peninsula

 Localised exchange → Pearl shells → Canoes

Torres Strait has no large trees for making canoes but it has lots of pearl shell, and Papua New Guinea has large trees. A special relationship formed between Torres Strait and nearby Papua New Guinea, where islanders exchanged their pearl shell for canoes and canoe hulls from Papua New Guinea. Some of this pearl shell also found its way through further networks of exchange to the highlands of Papua New Guinea.

Much of the movement of items between particular islands would have been based on kinship networks. Some other items exchanged between islands around 1904 include:

- pigments
- feathers
- garden foods
- harpoons
- bows and arrows
- red ochre
- drums
- sea foods
- wood for harpoons

Trading vessel from Papua New Guinea
Boigu, Torres Strait, 1989

Trading of certain goods is allowed between Papua New Guinea and some islands of Torres Strait under a treaty between Papua New Guinea and Australia. People from the nearby villages of Papua New Guinea often visit by watercraft to trade for goods that are more easily available in the island stores in the north of the strait.

CHAPTER 7

Shelter and housing

In pre-contact Australia, people lived in temporary or semi-permanent shelters. The shelters varied widely in size and were made from many different materials, including stone and the ribs of stranded whales. The types of shelters built depended on a range of things, such as:

- location
- season
- length of stay
- number of people
- ways that people organised themselves into household or family groups

Because of these changing factors, it was common for more than one type of shelter to be used in the one area.

Windbreaks and simple shelters were most common in desert regions. In colder and wetter regions, sturdier and more complex shelters were made. Semi-permanent and stone shelters were most likely to be built in locations that had a source of fresh water nearby.

FAST FACT

Names for temporary bush shelters include **humpy**, **gunyah**, **mia-mia** *and* **wurley**. *Different terms are found in different parts of the country.*

41

CHAPTER 7

SHELTER AND HOUSING

Forms of shelter Arnhem Land, NT

These illustrations show different types of shelters found in south-east Arnhem Land.

All of these shelters are built to cope with wet weather, except for shelter (a) which is used in the dry season and shelter (e).

Shelter (a) is a windbreak made of paperbark and supporting pegs. Shelter (b) uses folded pieces of tough bark sheets from a type of eucalyptus tree called the stringybark. It also has a raised ridge of earth surrounding the shelter to keep water out. Shelters (c) and (d) are both types of arched shelters that use poles to both raise and support the roof. The roof and walls are made from tough bark sheets of the stringybark.

All of the following shelters are designed to keep mosquitoes away. Shelter (e) is a raised platform with a fire underneath. Shelter (f) is a dome closed in on all sides with a small entry to help keep water out. Shelters (g), (h) and (i) are all types of arched shelters with a raised platform inside to keep people and their belongings off the ground.

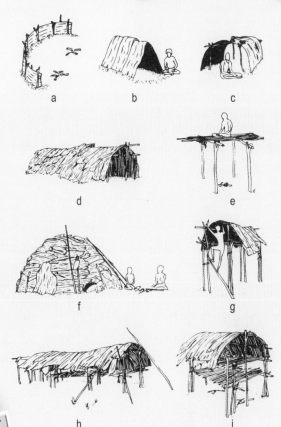

windbreak

A windbreak is something which provides protection from the wind, such as a fence or row of trees.

Framed shelters
Atherton area, Qld, 1918

In this area, shelters were made from pliable cane or branches tied together. The covering was of grass, leaves or bark.

Traditional round house covered with grass
Mer Island, Torres Strait, 1898

These distinctive beehive-shaped houses were made from a structure of bamboo poles tied together and then covered with lengths of grass. They were often between five and nine metres from side to side.

🔊 HOW DO YOU SAY IT?

Mer
mair

Remains of a stone house Lake Condah, Victoria

People often lived in large camps at certain times of the year in areas which had a good source of water. The people of Lake Condah built permanent houses with stone walls that they could return to each year to catch eels when they were in season. This photo shows the remains of one of those stone houses. The remains of an eel trap in this area are shown in Chapter 5.

Temporary and semi–permanent shelters have now mainly been replaced by the introduced European style of permanent housing. Most people now live in housing that is built to last for many years and is usually connected to a water and power supply.

CHAPTER 8

Fire

People made fire in two ways – either by friction or percussion. Friction is when pieces of wood are rubbed together to create smouldering wood powder. Percussion is when pieces of stone are hit together to create a spark. The smouldering wood powder or spark goes into dry material such as grass, leaves, shredded bark, feathers, hair or animal dung, which is called tinder. It is then blown on gently until it catches fire.

WORD ALERT

smoulders
If something smoulders, it burns slowly with smoke, but without flame.

Making fire

This map shows where the different ways of making fire were found across the country.

Friction was the most widespread type of making fire and could be done in three different ways.

///, The fire drill method was the most common way of making fire by friction. This method uses a hard stick of wood and a soft stick of wood which has a hollow in it. The hard stick sits in the hollow of the soft stick and is twisted very quickly between the palms until it creates smouldering wood powder. This is put into tinder and blown on gently until the tinder catches fire.

\\\\ The fire saw method uses the edge of a hard stick of wood or a spearthrower and a stick with a narrow opening or split. The hard stick or spearthrower is rubbed very quickly back and forth across the opening in the other stick until it creates smouldering wood powder. This is put into tinder and blown on gently until the tinder catches fire. The fire saw method was mainly found in the centre and north-west of the country.

≡ The fire plough method uses a hard stick of wood and soft stick of wood with a long groove in it. The hard stick is rubbed along a groove of the soft stick until it creates smouldering wood powder. This is put into tinder and blown on gently until the tinder catches fire. The fire plough method was only found in one area – the north-west of the country.

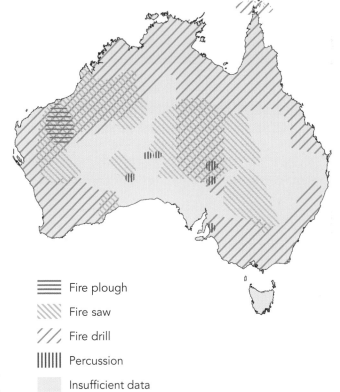

≡ Fire plough
\\\\ Fire saw
//, Fire drill
||||| Percussion
　 Insufficient data

The percussion method ||||||| was found in only a few small areas in the centre and south of the country. There is only one way of making fire with the percussion method. Here, pieces of stone are hit together to create a spark. The spark is created near the tinder and blown on gently until the tinder catches fire.

Making fire by one or more of these methods may also have been used elsewhere.

Teaching use of a fire drill
Arnhem Land, 2016

In this photo Traditional Owner Sam Gumgun shows Learning On Country students the technique of fire starting using the drill method.

WORD
ALERT

Traditional Owner
A Traditional Owner is an Indigenous Australian who has certain ties, rights and responsibilities for their lands.

For information on cultural burning as land management, see Chapter 19.

CHAPTER 9

Clothing and shell adornments

Clothing

Clothing was important as it provided protection from the weather. It was also a way to show differences in age, gender or group identities. Many different items of clothing were made and worn, including cloaks, rugs, skirts, belts and footwear. These were made from animal skins or plant materials such as bark, grass, reeds, pandanus leaves and even seaweed. Cloaks made from a number of pieces might be sewn together using bone needles. Sandals or moccasins were made from pieces of skins or bark sewn together. The string used in sewing was made from hair and fur.

Cloaks and footwear

This map shows where cloaks and footwear were worn. Cloaks were generally used only in the east and south-west of the continent. Skin cloaks were most common in the south where it is cooler, while cloaks from plant materials were used more in the north. Footwear ● was only found in small areas of the desert and Tasmania.

▨	Cloaks from skins
▨	Cloaks from plant material
●	Reports of footwear

Woman and child in a skin cloak
Lower Murray, SA, around 1869

In this photo, a woman is wearing a cloak with the fur on the outside. Cloaks were also worn with the fur on the inside, and the outside was sometimes decorated. In these cases, the outside had markings cut into them and ochre was rubbed onto the surface.

WORD ALERT

ochre

Ochre is a natural earth pigment, ranging in colour from pale yellow to red. Ochre had many uses, including decorating a person's body and wooden items.

Shell adornments

Shells were commonly worn as adornments in headbands, necklaces, pendants, nose ornaments and even as coverings for a person's groin area. The adornments were often worn during ceremonies. Sometimes, the shells would be decorated or engraved. The most common type of design was of geometric lines and shapes.

Items made from shell

The two most valued types of shell were bailer shells and pearl shells . Bailer shells are very large, curved shells belonging to a type of sea snail. They were called 'bailer' as they were used to bail water from canoes. Pearl shells belong to a type of oyster and have a glossy sheen to them.

Items made from bailer shell and pearl shell had widespread distribution. These two types of shell were traded from the north over a large area.

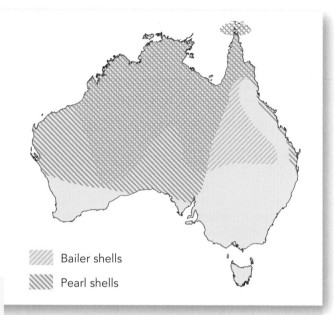

Bailer shells

Pearl shells

Men with pearl shell adornments Western Desert, 1970s

This photo shows young men dressed for a public ceremony at Jigalong in Western Australia. Two men in the middle are wearing engraved pearl shells hanging from belts made from hair around their waists. These shells would have come from the Kimberley, 900 kilometres away to the north.

Movement of pearl and bailer shells

This map shows the movement of pearl and bailer shells across the continent. These shells were highly valued and traded for other goods such as boomerangs, shields and ochre.

Pearl shells from the Kimberley made their way across much of the continent to the south and centre. Bailer shells from Cape York Peninsula made their way to the south of the continent.

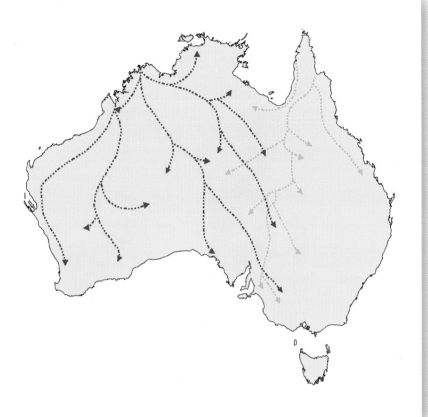

```
••• ►   Pearl shell
••• ►   Bailer shell
```

47

Bailer shell groin shield
Mer Island, Torres Strait, around 1900

This illustration shows a shield worn to protect the groin area. They were worn during warfare and ceremonies.

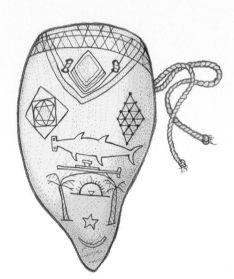

Pearl shell ornament Kimberley region, WA

This photo shows an engraved pearl shell ornament collected in 1931. The car may have belonged to the local Catholic bishop at the time this shell was decorated.

Women with pearl shell pendants Tudu Island, Torres Strait, around 1888

Two of the women in this photo are wearing pearl shell pendants. Their skirts are made from fibre.

Sacred Heart Church
Beagle Bay, WA

The Sacred Heart Church was built during World War I when Beagle Bay was a Catholic mission. This photo shows the altar inside of the church, which is nearly completely covered with pearl shell.

CHAPTER 10

Containers

A wide variety of containers were made from many different materials. Many of these are still made today. They could have different purposes depending on the materials used. The materials used to make a container often depended on the resources available in the local area. Materials included:

- animal skin
- bamboo
- bark
- cane
- grass

- hair
- leaves
- plant material
- shell
- wood

Further research is needed before some types of containers can be mapped completely.

Shell, leaf, bamboo and skin containers

This map shows that containers made from these materials are found in quite distinct regions. This is probably due to the availability of the materials and their intended use. Containers made from leaves ▨ were found in several locations. In Tasmania they were made from the leaves of a seaweed called bull kelp which is common there. Today these containers are made there as art objects. Skin containers ▨ were found mostly in the central and eastern parts of the country. As skin containers are relatively light, they were used in drier areas to carry water when people moved from place to place. Shell ▨ and bamboo ▨ containers were used mostly in the north. This may be because these materials were more available there than in the south.

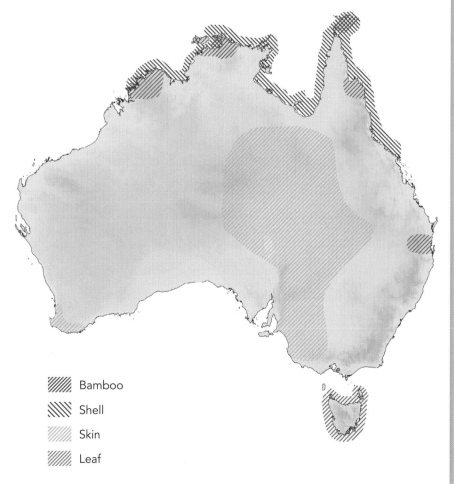

▨ Bamboo
▨ Shell
▨ Skin
▨ Leaf

Baskets were mainly used to hold and carry food and for storing personal items. They were made from weaving, plaiting or twisting together fibres of hair, bark, reeds, grass, leaves, and other materials. They could be woven so tightly that they could carry honey or liquids without leaking. Baskets seem to have been more common in the east and north of the continent.

Pandanus basket
Darwin region, NT, around 1877

This style of basket is made from the leaves of a pandanus plant. It is also known as a 'dillybag'. These baskets were used across the northern part of the Northern Territory, where this plant is mostly found. Today, these baskets are still an important part of ceremonial life but may also be made for sale.

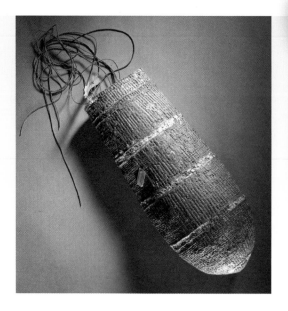

pandanus

The pandanus plant has long palm-like leaves which are ideal for making intricate baskets.

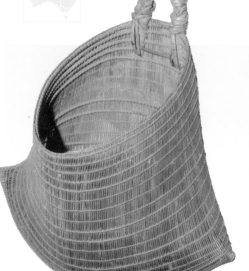

Bicornual split lawyer-cane basket Tully, Qld

This beautiful type of basket had many different uses, but it was only made in the southern part of the Queensland rainforest region where a type of tree called lawyer cane grows. It was used to carry food, catch small fish, and to clean plant foods by running water through it. It is called a 'bicornual' basket because it has two pointy 'horns' on the lower corners.

Bags were woven from string, handmade cord, or knotted grass stalks. Unlike baskets, they were generally collapsible. Some net-like bags could also stretch to hold more or larger items. They were mainly used for carrying food but were sometimes also used to carry small infants.

String bag
North-east Arnhem Land, NT, 1937

This photograph shows a person using a finely-woven string bag to sift seeds onto a large sheet of bark.

Wood and bark containers

We have limited information about the distribution of these kinds of containers. However, the information we do have shows that bark containers ▨ were found mostly across the north and down the south-east coast. Wooden containers ▧ were used mostly in the extreme west and near the centre of the country.

▨ Bark

▧ Wood

▢ Insufficient data

Bark bucket
Kimberley region, WA, around 1930

This bucket is made from two pieces of paperbark which are stitched together with handmade cord. Buckets like this were used to carry food and water.

Coolamon King Sound, WA, 1887

The coolamon is the iconic Indigenous wooden container that was used for many purposes, such as carrying bush foods, or in the past, for carrying a baby. It was the classic container in drier regions.

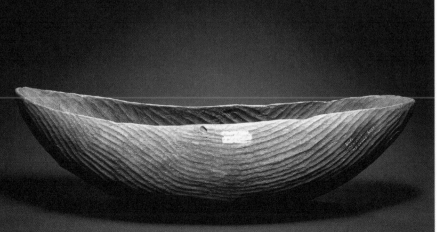

CHAPTER 11 Cultural and religious life

Cultural identification and activity

When the colonisation of Australia began, Indigenous societies and cultures varied considerably from place to place. In the east and south-west of the continent, non-Indigenous colonisers found an environment most like the one they had left behind. They established farms, industries, towns and cities, forcing Indigenous people to leave their lands and severely disrupting their way of life. In the north and centre of the continent, the colonisers arrived later and found land which was more difficult for them to use. Non-Indigenous settlement there was much less – as it still largely is today. Though colonisation in these areas also displaced Indigenous people, it caused relatively less disruption to their cultural life.

A survey was done in 2014–2015 called the National Aboriginal and Torres Strait Islander Social Survey – NATSISS for short. It included questions about cultural life. The following three maps show some of the results from the survey. Comparing the maps, we see a very similar pattern across the country, with the highest rates all being in the remote north and west. This suggests that there is a connection or relationship between these culturally significant parts of life:

- identifying with a cultural group
- being involved in cultural activities
- being able to meet cultural obligations

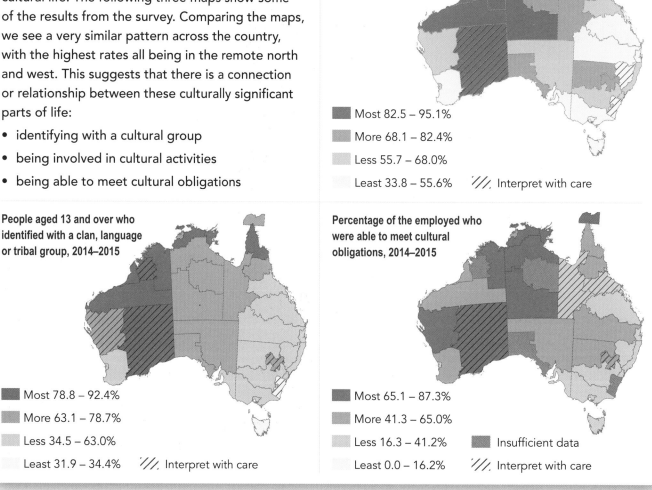

People aged 13 years and over who were involved with cultural activities or Indigenous organisations, 2014–2015

Most 82.5 – 95.1%
More 68.1 – 82.4%
Less 55.7 – 68.0%
Least 33.8 – 55.6%   /// Interpret with care

People aged 13 and over who identified with a clan, language or tribal group, 2014–2015

Most 78.8 – 92.4%
More 63.1 – 78.7%
Less 34.5 – 63.0%
Least 31.9 – 34.4%   /// Interpret with care

Percentage of the employed who were able to meet cultural obligations, 2014–2015

Most 65.1 – 87.3%
More 41.3 – 65.0%
Less 16.3 – 41.2%   ▪ Insufficient data
Least 0.0 – 16.2%   /// Interpret with care

Initiation

Both men and women were involved in rites and ceremonies throughout their lives. Over most of the continent, initiation rites which marked the transition between boyhood and manhood were the focus of large ceremonies. These involved activities over a number of days that celebrated ancestral events with song, dance and painting. Girls went through fewer and less elaborate rites moving from girlhood to womanhood.

Male initiation ceremonies

A common part of a male initiation ceremony was to change part of the initiate's body. This happened in a number of ways. Circumcision and subincision \\\\\ are the most common forms and are found over a large part of the continent. Removing some front teeth is found mainly in the south-east. Over some much smaller areas, some body hair was removed \\\\\, scars were made on the body, or the nose was pierced \\\\\. In parts of Western Australia and Queensland, it is unclear if any changes to the body were part of the initiation.

WORD ALERT

circumcision

Circumcision is the practice of cutting away the skin around the end of the penis, usually for religious or cultural reasons.

subincision

Subincision is a similar practice where a cut is made from the tip of the underside of the penis downwards.

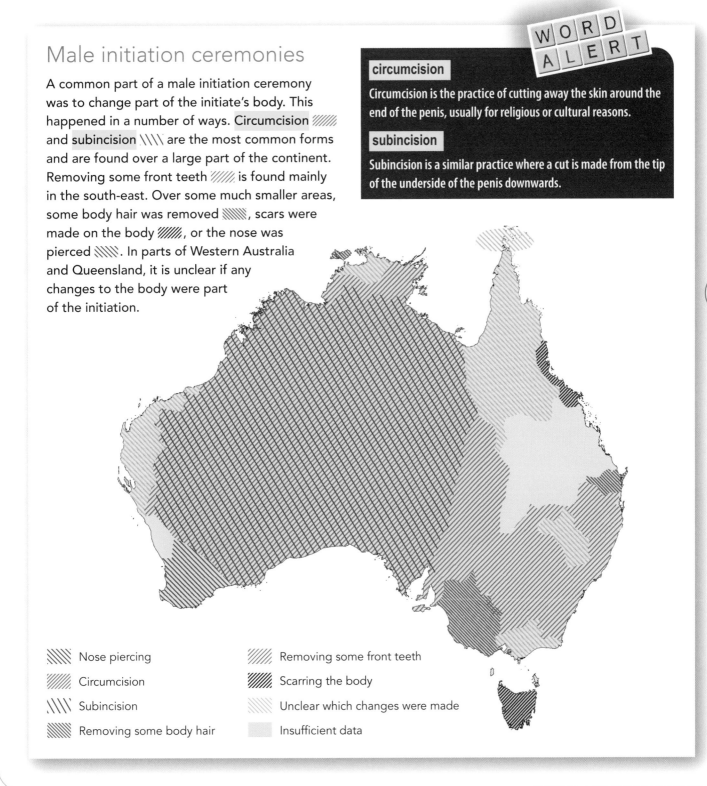

\\\\\ Nose piercing		Removing some front teeth	
Circumcision		Scarring the body	
\\\\\ Subincision		Unclear which changes were made	
Removing some body hair		Insufficient data	

The journeys of two initiates around 1977 and 1994

Another part of male initiation in the central desert is to take boys on a journey to gather people together for their circumcision ceremony. In the past they went by foot, and the journey could last several months. More recently, motor vehicles and aeroplanes have greatly increased the range of these journeys and the size of the ceremonies. The 1977 journey began at Papunya ■ and the initiate and his guardian travelled by car. For the 1994 journey, the initiate and his guardian first flew from Tjuntjuntjara ■ to Alice Springs and then to Willowra. From there they continued by car to Lajamanu. By the time they returned to Tjuntjuntjara they had gathered a convoy of more than 30 vehicles and over 400 people. Both journeys covered vast distances and crossed state borders, showing the extent and strength of desert kinship networks.

◄))) HOW DO YOU SAY IT?

Tjuntjuntjara
joon-juhn-**jah**-ruh

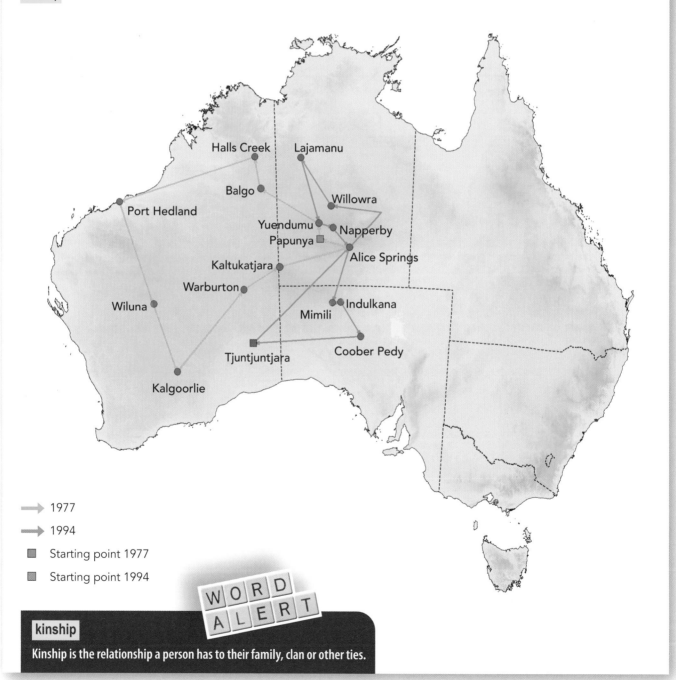

⟶ 1977

⟶ 1994

■ Starting point 1977

■ Starting point 1994

WORD ALERT

kinship

Kinship is the relationship a person has to their family, clan or other ties.

Boys being painted before circumcision

North-east Arnhem Land, NT, 2003

Body paintings are a feature of circumcision ceremonies in north-east Arnhem Land. The painted designs on the chest of each boy belong to the boy's clan or to his grandmother's clan. These same designs are often used today on bark paintings made for sale.

Man with scarification

Mt Barnett, WA, around 1911

This photo shows a man with ritual scarring running across his chest. This is also called scarification.

Introduced religions

Indigenous belief systems centre around the creator ancestral beings. These beings:

- gave form to the land, waters and sea
- created or gave birth to the first humans
- laid down the laws and languages

Christianity first came to Indigenous Australia in the 1820s in the form of missionary societies rather than churches. They attempted to replace Indigenous beliefs and practices with Christian beliefs. These early missionary societies were mostly in the south of the continent.

FAST FACT

There were many different branches of Christianity – all with different names:

Anglican, Apostolic, Baptist, Catholic, Congregational, Lutheran, Methodist, Pentecostal, Presbyterian

Expansion of missions, 1870s–1960s

From the late 1800s a large number of branches of Christianity expanded to cover many parts of the country. In 1865, Presbyterian, Methodist and Congregational religious societies joined with the colonial governments to convert large areas of northern Australia into reserves controlled by missions. In the 1880s, Catholic, Lutheran and Anglican societies joined this process. Torres Strait was first converted by the London Missionary Society in 1871, then in 1914 it came under the control of the Anglicans. A last wave of missionary activity created the Aborigines Inland Mission and the United Aborigines Mission.

 Catholic

 Anglican

 ● Presbyterian

 ● Lutheran

 Methodist

 Baptist

 ● Aborigines Inland Mission

 United Aborigines Mission

 Apostolic Church of Australia

||||||| London Missionary Society

○ Church of Christ

● Christian Brethren

Obelisk at Saibai Island Church
Torres Strait, 1989

The arrival of the London Missionary Society in Torres Strait in 1871 is known as 'The Coming of the Light'. This is represented by the obelisk in this photo, which is a lighthouse set on the top of an outrigger canoe.

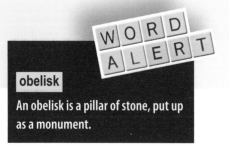

obelisk
An obelisk is a pillar of stone, put up as a monument.

Christian and Pentecostal missions, 1970s–1993

Following World War II some churches began to hand back mission lands and properties to Indigenous peoples. In Arnhem Land in the late 1970s, Yolngu Christians combined Indigenous and other forms of Christianity. The Elcho Island Revival of 1979 led to a series of crusades across the country during 1982–1993. At this same time, Indigenous leaders in the Aborigines Inland Mission and United Aborigines Mission rejected the non-Indigenous control of churches and formed the Aboriginal Evangelical Fellowship, which became active in the south of the country. Pentecostalism has continued to expand over the Kimberley and parts of Queensland. Today, people often practise both Christian and Indigenous Australian religions.

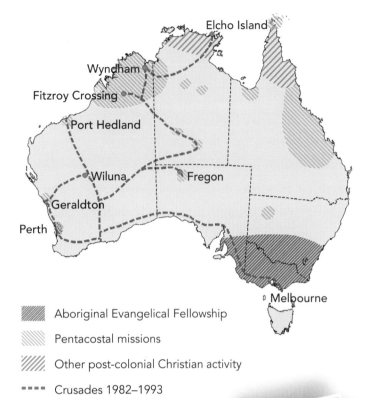

Aboriginal Evangelical Fellowship

Pentacostal missions

Other post-colonial Christian activity

- - - - Crusades 1982–1993

🔊 **HOW DO YOU SAY IT?**

Yolngu
yool–ngooh

crusade
A crusade is an expedition to spread the word of Christianity.

WORD ALERT

CHAPTER 12 Performing arts

Before contact with Europeans, Indigenous music, song and dance were central in performances that celebrated the travels and activities of ancestral beings. In many parts of Australia this tradition continues to flourish. Indigenous music today is rich and vibrant and covers a wide range of styles and sounds. Indigenous Australians are outstanding in Australia's performing arts world in many roles – as writers, directors, actors, choreographers, musicians and dancers.

Musical instruments

Traditionally, music was largely vocal. Instruments were mainly used to create rhythms to accompany songs and dances rather than creating melodies in their own right. Instruments had to be portable and easily replaced if lost. Most instruments were made of wood and some, such as boomerangs, were everyday items with other uses.

The didgeridoo

The most iconic of Indigenous instruments is the didgeridoo. It was originally found only in Arnhem Land, the Kimberley and the northern Pilbara 〰️. It has now spread throughout Australia and is played almost everywhere 〰️. It has also become popular with musicians overseas. The map also shows that the didgeridoo is not played in Torres Strait 〰️.

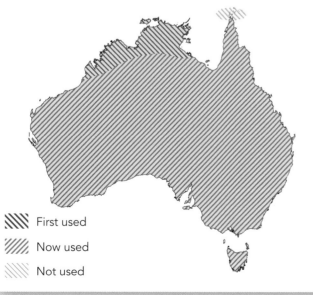

First used

Now used

Not used

The didgeridoo in a dance performance
North-east Arnhem Land, NT, 1974
The instrument is usually made from a hollow tree that has been eaten out by termites. The inside is smoothed out and gum resin is added at the narrower end to form a mouthpiece. In this photo, a metal container is being used at the base of the didgeridoo to amplify the sound.

Boomerangs and clapsticks

Two of the most widely used instruments were pairs of boomerangs ● and clapsticks ◆ that were struck against each other. In some cases, boomerangs were rattled together at their tips. The beating of sticks on the ground ■ was found mostly in the centre and west. Clapsticks accompanying the didgeridoo ▲ were found in the north.

- ● Boomerangs
- ▲ Didgeridoo and clapsticks (beaten by singer)
- ◆ Clapsticks only
- ■ Stick beaten on ground

WORD ALERT

clapsticks

Clapsticks are short sticks of hard wood which are struck against each other to create a rhythm.

CHAPTER 12

PERFORMING ARTS

59

The body as an instrument

Clapping hands ● and the slapping of the thighs ■ or lap ▲ were found over much of the continent. These were other ways of forming rhythmic sounds. Women slapped their laps and men slapped their thighs. Thigh slapping by men seems to have been confined to the western side of the Top End.

- ● Hand clapping
- ▲ Lap slapping (women)
- ■ Thigh slapping (men)

WORD ALERT

Top End

The Top End is another name for the northern part of the NT.

Rasps

Rasps are a percussion instrument consisting of two parts:

1 a solid block or carved piece of wood with a serrated surface

2 a stick or wooden rod

The stick or wooden rod is scraped over the wood to create the sound. This map shows that rasps were limited mostly to the central west of Western Australia.

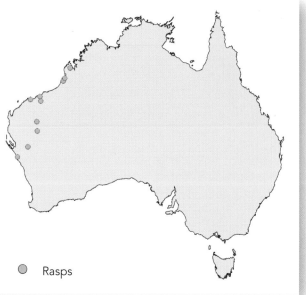

● Rasps

'Butcher' Joe Nangan playing a rasp
Kimberley Region, WA

Some rasps could be used for more than one purpose. A spearthrower with notches along the top could also be used as a rasp. These were scraped with a stick. Others, like the rasp in this photo, were specially made to be played just as an instrument.

FAST FACT

Goanna skin was often used for the top of skin drums.

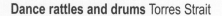

Dance rattles and drums Torres Strait

Torres Strait rattles are made from various kinds of beans or nuts, and attached to handles made of wood or string. The drums illustrated here were made in Torres Strait, but these types are also imported from Papua New Guinea.

Bark and skin bundles, logs, drums and rattles

Mostly in the south of the continent, women accompanied songs by hitting bark bundles or pillows ▲ made of animal skin. Skin drums ⊙, hollow logs or canoes hit with sticks ◆ ■, and rattles ⬟ were mostly found in Torres Strait and nearby Cape York Peninsula. Drums from Papua New Guinea also found their way to Cape York.

- ⊙ Skin drum struck with open palm or stick
- ▲ Bark or skin bundle beaten, or struck on ground
- ■ Hollow log (or canoe) struck with paired sticks
- ◆ Hollow log struck with small stick
- ⬟ Seed rattles

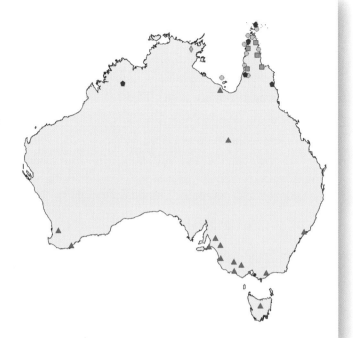

Whistles

Most whistles were used to create sounds or melodies and could be made from various materials. Leaf whistles ▲ became popular in the early to mid-1900s in the south-east of the country. These were used to play melodies such as hymns and folk tunes. Whistles made from bone and reed ⊙ were found in Torres Strait and Cape York Peninsula.

Whistles could also be used for another reason. The leaf whistles ▲ found on Cape York Peninsula were used as danger signals. The sound travelled far enough to warn of unknown or unwanted persons approaching.

- ⊙ Bone or reed whistle
- ▲ Folded leaf whistle

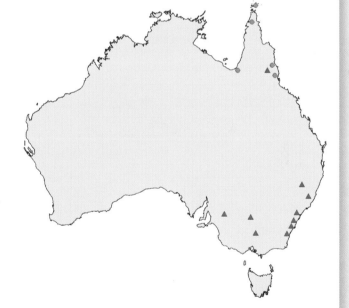

Gumleaf players Lake Tyers, Victoria, 1930s

Gumleaf bands used to travel and perform throughout New South Wales and Victoria.

Indigenous music today is broad and diverse. It is just as likely to be heard on national radio or in the Sydney Opera House as in remote community festivals or around a camp fire. Songs are passed on in local languages. Indigenous language, melodies, rhythms and stories with Country are also melded with rock, classical, and even hip-hop.

Groups such as Yothu Yindi, The Lonely Boys and Warumpi Band, and solo artists such as Gurrumul, Archie Roach, Jessica Mauboy, Briggs, Deborah Cheetham and Dan Sultan appeal to a wide audience both here and overseas.

Classical music composer Brenda Gifford at the piano

Brenda Gifford is a composer and classically trained saxophonist, pianist and teacher. She has played with Aboriginal musicians such as Bart Willoughby and Kev Carmody. She has also collected over 100 oral histories of Aboriginal musicians.

Some festivals and events featuring Indigenous music, 2018

The majority of festivals and events that are mapped here focus on celebrating local Indigenous culture and community. Indigenous music and dance are also key parts of other festivals, such as the Desert Song Festival, Big Sound and the Furneaux Islands Festival. Some of these festivals have existed for decades, while new ones seem to appear every year. These events are concentrated in the Northern Territory, New South Wales and Victoria.

1   The Coming of the Light Festival
2   Winds of Zenadth
3   Laura Dance Festival
4   Big Sound
5   Boomerang Festival
6   Festival of Baiame's Ngunnhu
7   Saltwater Freshwater Festival
8   Aboriginal Cultural Showcase
9   Yabun Festival
10 Homeground Festival
11 Share the Spirit Festival
12 Yirramboi Festival
13 Yalukut Weela, Ngargee
14 Tarerer Festival
15 Furneaux Islands Festival
16 Nayri Niara (Good Spirit) Festival
17 Putalina Festival
18 Spirit Festival
19 Garma Festival
20 Barunga Festival
21 Walking with Spirits Festival
22 Desert Harmony Festival
23 Big Sing in the Desert
24 Desert Song Festival
25 Tjungu Festival
26 Wardarnji Aboriginal Cultural Festival

Dance

Traditional dance has not been studied as much as song. Dances are usually re-enactments of ancestral events or representations of ancestral beings. They are sometimes sacred and not shared with outsiders. Dance styles of men and women vary widely across the continent.

The dance of the dugong hunters
North-east Arnhem Land, NT, 2003

This dance re-enacts an ancestral dugong hunt. It is being performed as part of a burial ceremony. The harpooning of the dugong represents capturing the deceased person's spirit so that it can return to the spirit world of the ancestors. Men usually take centre stage and the women dance on the edges in Arnhem Land ceremonial dances.

dugong
A dugong is a plant-eating water mammal with front limbs like flippers.

WORD ALERT

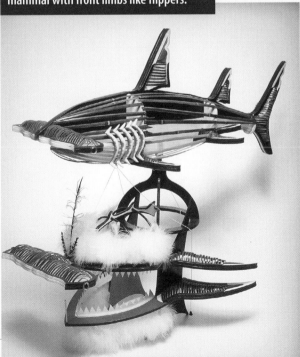

Torres Strait dancers Torres Strait, 2004

Torres Strait dancing is often performed in rows. Dancers wear grass skirts and use distinctive masks with moving parts that represent the topics of the dance. Some dance styles show a strong South Pacific influence. Dances can be traditional or new and take recent events as their theme.

This photo shows a dance where events of World War II are being re-enacted. Their head decorations are models of war planes.

Beizam (hammerhead shark) dance mask
Artist: Ken Thaiday Sr, 1994

Ken Thaiday was commissioned by art galleries and museums to produce spectacular dance masks featuring moving parts, such as this hammerhead shark mask.

Today, Indigenous dance remains a main feature of community events and performing arts festivals. Companies such as Bangarra Dance Theatre, Koomurri and Blakdance have melded traditional forms of dance with Western dance. Touring companies perform these new styles across Australia and overseas. Many of these companies also visit schools to work with children.

Film and television

Indigenous Australians were largely invisible to movie audiences until 1955 when the film *Jedda* was released. Since that time Indigenous actors such as David Gulpilil, Deborah Mailman, Tom E. Lewis and Justine Saunders have produced some of the most memorable and powerful performances in Australian film. Film directors like Ivan Sen (*Toomelah*, 2011), Rachel Perkins (*Bran Nue Dae*, 2009) and Warwick Thornton (*Samson and Delilah*, 2009) are highly regarded in Australia and overseas.

Original poster for *Jedda* 1955

This groundbreaking film starred Rosalie Kunoth-Monks (formerly Ngarla Kunoth) and Robert Tudawali. It was produced and directed by Charles Chauvel. It was the first Australian feature film to employ Indigenous actors in the lead roles.

We Don't Need a Map poster 2017

A thought-provoking documentary by award-winning Aboriginal director Warwick Thornton, *We Don't Need a Map*, looks at the very different meanings Indigenous and non-Indigenous Australians associate with the Southern Cross constellation.

🔊 HOW DO YOU SAY IT?

Yuendumu
yooh-uhn-duh-**mooh**

Indigenous involvement in Australian television began with the Broadcasting for Remote Aboriginal Communities Scheme (BRACS) trialled in Ernabella and Yuendumu in the late 1980s. This was followed by the Imparja network serving remote communities in the late 1990s. Australians now enjoy Indigenous-produced programs through the National Indigenous Television (NITV) network. NITV has produced a number of award-winning shows, including:

- *Redfern Now* – drama
- *First Australians* – documentary series
- *Marngrook Footy Show* – sports talk show
- *Little J and Big Cuz* – children's show
- *The Point* – news and current affairs

Art

Australian Indigenous art extends over thousands of years and is one of the great world art traditions. Rock art in Australia is at least as old as the earliest art in Europe. Current work by Indigenous artists is highly valued and makes a major contribution to the world art scene. Its strength comes from a deep spiritual identity with the land and the sea.

WORD ALERT

ochre

Ochre is a natural earth pigment, ranging in colour from pale yellow to red. Ochre had many uses, including decorating a person's body and wooden items.

Dreamtime

The Dreamtime is the time in which Aboriginal people believe the earth came to have its current form and in which life and nature began.

Rock art

The earliest art was paintings or engravings on boulders or on the walls of rock shelters and caves. Some early cave sites just contain finger markings. Art was probably brought to Australia by the first Indigenous settlers between 65 000 and 50 000 years ago. The archaeological record in central Australia shows that people were mining red ochre there 30 000 years ago – probably for use as paint.

People often associate these very old images with the actions of ancestral beings, and consider them sacred. They may retouch them as a way of expressing their spiritual connections with the Dreamtime.

Where rock art styles are found

The rock art of Australia has been grouped into four broad styles.

🔊 HOW DO YOU SAY IT?

Panaramitee
pan–uh–ram–uh–tee

● Finger markings are lines made on a soft surface such as limestone. They are found in deep caves across the south coast of the continent.

● The early **Panaramitee** style was made up of engravings on rock. They are found widely across the continent and feature markings of circles, lines, arcs, animal tracks and dots.

▦ The simple figurative style consisted of painted or engraved silhouettes of human and animal forms. It is found mostly in the north-west, north and east of the continent. Figurative art may offer early evidence for strong spiritual links between Indigenous groups and ancestral beings that have animal forms.

▧ The complex figurative style of painting developed later in the tropical north, and the Kimberley and Pilbara regions. It was more detailed than the simple figurative style and included 'x-ray' paintings which showed the internal structure and organs of living things.

WORD ALERT

figurative

A figurative painting is of the form or figure of a human or animal.

silhouette

A silhouette is a drawing which has an outer line filled in, like a shadow.

Finger markings
Koonalda Cave, SA

This photo shows finger markings made in the soft limestone of Koonalda Cave in South Australia. They were made about 30 000 years ago.

🔊 HOW DO YOU SAY IT? Murujuga **moo**–roo–joo–gah

Engravings in the Panaramitee style
Victoria River region, NT

The engravings shown in this photo are made up of circles and lines. Other common designs of the Panaramitee style are arcs, animal tracks and dots.

Engraved figure in the simple figurative style
Burrup Peninsula, WA

The Burrup Peninsula is also called Murujuga. The rock engravings on the peninsula and nearby islands make up one of the most significant areas of rock art in the world. There are over 1 million engravings. The earliest are around 45 000 years old, and the latest date to the 1800s. This photo shows an engraved figure found in Murujuga.

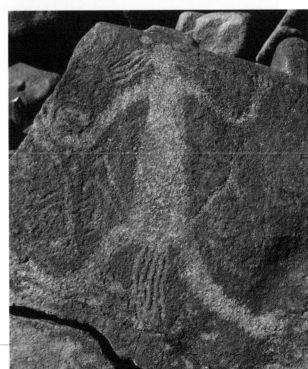

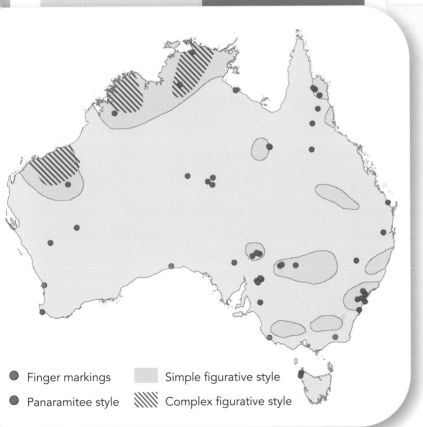

● Finger markings   Simple figurative style

● Panaramitee style   ▨ Complex figurative style

Gwion Gwion / Gwion figures in the simple figurative style North Kimberley, WA

Gwion Gwion and *Gwion* are Wunambal, Worrorra and Ngarinyin (closely related Australian Aboriginal languages) names for this style of rock art. The Gwion Gwion and Gwion style features red ochre painted human figures. They are often shown wearing items such as headdresses, belts, tassels and bags, as well as carrying hunting tools such as boomerangs, spears and spearthrowers.

🔊 **HOW DO YOU SAY IT?**

Gwion
gwee–yon
or **gwee**–yahn

Dynamic figure in the simple figurative style Near Gunbalanya, western Arnhem Land, NT

'Dynamic' was introduced as a term to describe this early figurative style in Arnhem Land. The figures are often grouped together in scenes showing activities connected to ceremony, hunting or fighting. People today identify these figures as 'mimi' – spirits that are said to live inside the rock.

🔊 **HOW DO YOU SAY IT?**

Gunbalanya
gahn–buh–lahn–juh

Painting in the x-ray style, complex figurative style Near Gunbalanya, western Arnhem Land, NT

In Arnhem Land, figures began to be shown with their bone structures and hollow places within the body. This style was called 'x-ray' art as it showed the inside of a living thing. In later periods, x-ray art was used to show internal organs – not just bone structures and hollow places. Most x-ray paintings were of fish.

69

Painting of Wanjina figure in the complex figurative style North Kimberley, WA

In the Kimberley, Wanjina figures, also written Wandjina or also known as Gulingi (from closely related languages Worrorra, Wunambal and Ngarinyin) depicted in rock paintings throughout the Wanjina Wunggurr Community's country are the supreme creators and symbols of fertility and rain. Wanjina have no mouth but their different headdress and body styles and adornments, such as pearl shell pendants, signify purpose. The Kaiaira Wanjina (pictured) are associated with creating and looking after saltwater and coastal places and the Gulingi Wanjina (Wunambal Gaambera language) are associated with lightning and rain.

🔊 HOW DO YOU SAY IT?

Wanjina
wond–jin–uh
or **wond**–jin–ah

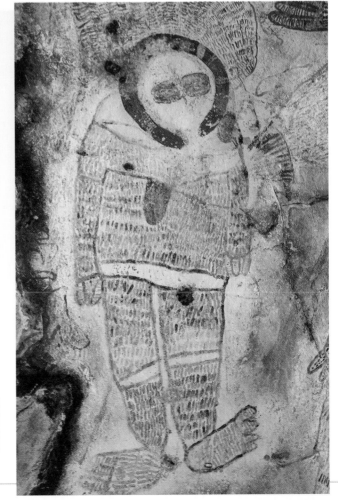

Carved trees

Carved trees were trees which had their bark stripped off and patterns cut into them. They were associated with burial sites and initiation sites. It is not known when the tradition first started. Most surviving examples show marks from metal tools, and so must have been carved in the 1800s.

Area where carved trees are found

The practice of carving trees was concentrated in New South Wales and south-east Queensland.

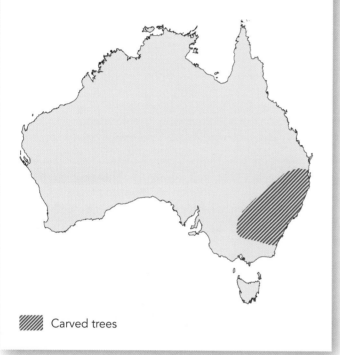

▨ Carved trees

A carved tree Near Molong, NSW
This photo shows the trunk of a carved tree.

FAST FACT

The famous Arrernte artist Albert Namatjira was trained in watercolour painting in 1936. His work led to the rise of the 'Hermannsburg School' of landscape painting.

Modern art

By the 1960s and 1970s, interest in Indigenous art had grown and a strong market for Indigenous artworks began to develop. Many communities opened art and craft centres in response to this demand. Individual artists became recognised and new forms of art were created, including the following:

- painting
- sculpture
- basketmaking
- ceramics
- photography
- printmaking
- fabric printing
- glassmaking
- shell jewellery

Art and craft centres, 2017

Art centres are generally organisations that are not formed mainly for the purpose of making a profit. They are often owned jointly by the artists themselves. The centres employ staff to encourage artists and supply them with materials. The staff also purchase, document, and market the works.

Many art centres are connected to larger organisations that support, promote and advocate for their activities. This map shows the coverage of two organisations that operate in remote regions – the Association of Northern, Kimberley and Arnhem Aboriginal Artists (ANKAAA) ● and Desart ●. This map also shows that the Indigenous art and craft industry operates across the whole country.

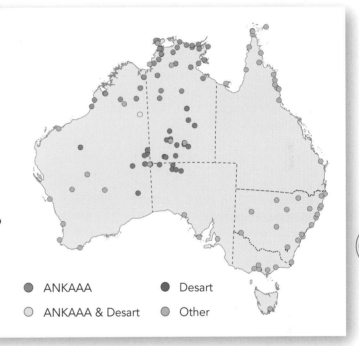

- ● ANKAAA
- ○ ANKAAA & Desart
- ● Desart
- ● Other

🔊 HOW DO YOU SAY IT?

Tingarri
ting-guh-ree

Kirij
ki-rij

Tjukala
jook-uh-lah

Tingarri* men travelling from *Kirij* to *Tjukala

Artist: John Tjakamarra, 1991

The earlier Panaramitee style has remained important in the desert regions, and has been called the oldest continuous art style in the world. The style continues the tradition of using dots, circles and tracks but these are now painted on canvas. This style of art is now known as 'desert art'.

72

Mina-Mina ceremonies at Kimayi

Artist: Nancy Naninurra, 1997

This artwork is another example of the desert art style.

🔊 **HOW DO YOU SAY IT?**

Kimayi
kim–uy

The female rainbow serpent beneath waterlilies in her sacred billabong

Artist: Lofty Bardayal Nadjamerrek, 1991

Western Arnhem Land paintings often show birds, fish and plant foods. This painting shows the powerful ancestral being – the rainbow serpent. The artist has also included several other features such a crocodile, emu, snake and fish. Waterlilies and a palm tree are attached to the serpent's back. At sacred places, these plants are a sign that the rainbow serpent is there in the land or under the water.

Landscapes at Kalumpiwarra, Yalmanta and Ngulalintji Artist: Rover Thomas, 1984

A new art style in the Kimberley region is where artists recreate early rock paintings on bark or plywood to show features of the Kimberley landscape. Rover Thomas is perhaps the best known artist from the Kimberley and was one of the founders of this landscape tradition.

Spirit figure with wallaby Artist: Dundiwuy Wanambi, 1987

Yolngu artists from north-east Arnhem Land make sculptures that represent ancestral beings. This art is linked to their clans, the system of land ownership, and each clan has its own design. The artist's clan design is painted on the chest of the ancestral being shown here.

◀ HOW DO YOU SAY IT?

Kalumpiwarra
kah-**loom**-pee-wah-ruh

Yalmanta
yahl-mun-tuh

Ngulalintji
ngoo-luh-**lin**-chee

Yolngu
yool-ngooh

WORD ALERT

clan

A clan is a group of people who are related by descent from a common ancestor.

Emarr Totol   Artist: Erub Arts collaboration, 2017

Emarr Totol is a fine example of a 'ghost net' being used in a sculpture. A ghost net is a lost or abandoned fishing net which drifts with the currents and sometimes washes up on shore. They are a danger to marine life as species such as turtles get caught in them and drown.

This type of artwork shows the growing awareness of the environmental and conservation issues Indigenous people face because of global and unprofessional fishing practices.

Arrkutja errintja *(wild woman)*
Artist: Irene Mpitjaana Entata, 1995

Female potters of Hermannsburg in the Northern Territory now make bright and striking terracotta pottery and ceramic tiles. The pottery artworks feature landscapes which are a traditional style of Hermannsburg painting.

🔊 **HOW DO YOU SAY IT?**

Emarr Totol
em–ahr **toh**–tohl

Arrkutja errintja
ahr–kooch–uh
e–rin–juh

Sports

Indigenous Australians have excelled in sports introduced by non–Indigenous Australians since the mid–1860s. Since 1962, a total of 68 Indigenous athletes have represented Australia in the Olympic Games. Over this time Indigenous Olympians have won 14 medals in sports such as swimming, hockey, basketball, and athletics.

The first Australian cricket team to tour England, 1868

Some Aboriginal people learnt to play cricket when working as station hands in western Victoria. This photograph is of the first Australian cricket team to tour England. The majority of the team was made up of Aboriginal players. The team won 14 games, drew 19 and lost 14.

10 Wills's arrival with the team, photographed at the Albert Ground, Sydney, February 1867. This Club was founded in 1861. According to a record in Lord's historical collection, the team members are: at rear (left to right)—Tarpot, T. W. Wills, Mullagh; front row—King Cole (leg on chair), Dick-a-Dick; seated (left to right)—Jellico, Peter, Red Cap, Harry Rose, Bullocky, Cuzens.

Indigenous players in AFL, netball and NRL

This chart shows the proportion of Indigenous players in AFL, netball and NRL in each state. The proportion of AFL players is highest in the north, south and west of the country. The proportion of NRL players is highest in the east and north-east of the country. Netball players are represented across the country. Both AFL and NRL are dominated by boys and men, whereas netball is dominated by girls and women. Increasingly, girls and women are becoming more involved in playing both AFL and NRL.

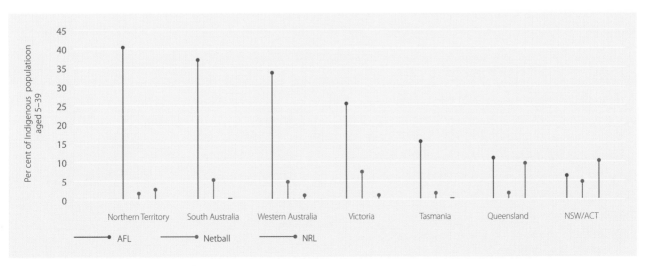

Birthplace of male NRL and AFL Indigenous All Stars, 2015

Every year, the National Rugby League (NRL) and the Australian Football League (AFL) each name a team of their top performing Indigenous players. The players who are chosen for these teams are called All Stars. Before the start of each football season, each All Stars team plays another team within their competition as a display match. This map, showing where these players were born, also reflects where each sport is mostly played.

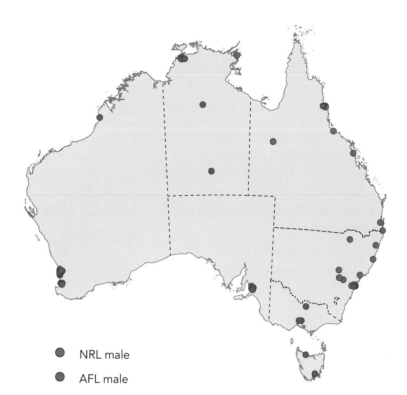

● NRL male
● AFL male

FAST FACT

marngrook

It is likely that the game we know today as AFL had its origins not only in Gaelic Football but also in the game of marngrook. Versions of marngrook were found across the country at the time of colonisation. It involved a number of players kicking and catching a ball made from stuffed animal skin.

Birthplace of female NRL Indigenous All Stars, 2015

The first female Indigenous All Stars team for the NRL was named in 2011. This map, showing where the 2015 All Star players were born, also reflects the popularity of the sport in Queensland and New South Wales.

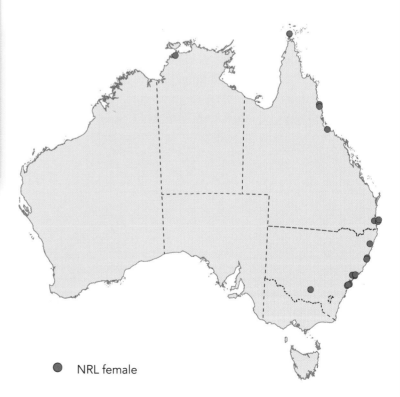

● NRL female

The Lajamanu Blues Aussie Rules team Yuendumu Sports Weekend, NT, 2003

Indigenous people regularly have their own sporting carnivals. These are important social events, with people coming in from many different places to participate and watch. The president of the Yuendumu community council in the Northern Territory said the 2003 sports carnival was like a 'modern day corroboree'.

WORD ALERT

corroboree

A corroboree is an Aboriginal dance ceremony which includes singing and rhythmic music. The word comes from Dharug, a language of NSW.

🔊 HOW DO YOU SAY IT?

Yuendumu
yooh-uhn-duh-**mooh**

Nicky Winmar
Melbourne Cricket Ground, Victoria, 1993

Nicky Winmar is a former AFL player. In this photo, he shows his chest and points to his black skin at the Melbourne Cricket Ground. This was in response to racial abuse from the crowd during a game. All major sporting codes now have anti-racism policies in place. However, many Indigenous athletes are still subjected to racist taunts and actions.

Cathy Freeman with the Aboriginal flag
Victoria, Canada, 1994

Cathy Freeman is one of Australia's most famous athletes. This photo shows her running a lap of honour holding the Aboriginal flag after winning the 400 metres in the 1994 Commonwealth Games in Canada. Australian team officials criticised her for doing this, but she had wide support from the Australian public. Cathy went on to win the same event at the 2000 Olympics in Sydney.

Increasing numbers of Indigenous athletes have taken up long–distance running in recent years. Many have competed both across Australia and overseas with the mentoring of Robert de Castella and the support of the Indigenous Marathon Foundation.

Where graduates of the Indigenous Marathon Project live, 2018

The Indigenous Marathon Project was founded in 2009. It began with the training of four Indigenous men in long-distance running so they could compete in the New York City Marathon. All four men successfully finished the race despite having no running experience before their training. The Indigenous Marathon Project now has 75 graduates from communities across Australia who have finished major international marathons. These include marathons in New York, Boston, Tokyo, London, Paris and Berlin. The map shows where 60 of these graduates live, with many in the Top End of the Northern Territory, New South Wales, and Far North Queensland.

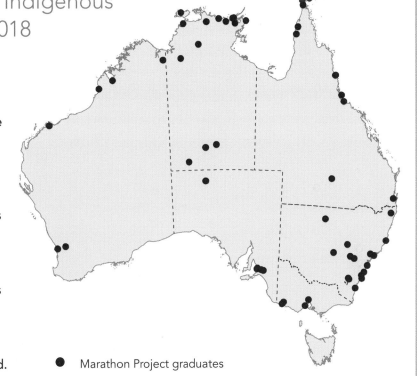

● Marathon Project graduates

Indigenous marathon runners at the completion of the New York City Marathon USA, 2017

From left to right, this photo shows:

- Indigenous Marathon Project coach Adrian Dodson-Shaw (Broome)
- Runner Maletta Seriat (Thursday Island)
- Runner Scott Cox (Broome)
- Runner Natasha Leslie (Karratha)
- Former world champion marathon runner and Indigenous Marathon Foundation Director Robert de Castella

Games and toys

In daily life, people had time for play. The games of pre-contact Australia were similar to those found in other parts of the world. There were team games involving handmade balls that were kicked, thrown or hit with some kind of stick. There were games that closely resembled marbles and bowling. There were throwing games that sometimes involved toys made specifically for the purpose. Spinning tops were popular in some areas, as were games that resembled board games. These games were usually played on the ground with stone counters. String games have been reported from many parts of the continent. In Torres Strait, men held model boat races.

While children's play activities are recreational, they also provide a foundation for learning and improving skills that are needed as an adult.

Men spinning tops

Mer Island, Torres Strait, around 1900

Tops were a common form of toy in Torres Strait. The ones shown here are made from ground stone but they could be made from a number of materials. Men on Mer held competitions to see who could spin their top for the longest.

FAST FACT

Racing model outrigger canoes in Torres Strait is still a popular activity with men today!

🔊 HOW DO YOU SAY IT?

Mer
mair

Balls woven from **pandanus leaf** Torres Strait

These plaited hollow balls were used in a children's game of 'catch'. Across the continent balls were made from a wide variety of materials. They also came in many shapes and sizes.

WORD ALERT

pandanus

The pandanus plant has long palm-like leaves which are ideal for making things like baskets and toys.

Throwing toy Dunk Island, Qld, collected in 1911

This toy imitates the flight of a returning boomerang when thrown. It is about 20 cm long and made from a folded pandanus leaf.

Motor car toys Arnhem Land, NT, 1980

Children in many places have been making toys like these since the 1940s. They were made from tins, wire, string and other readily available materials. The cars in this photo are made from two tobacco tins fixed to each end of a short piece of wood. The wood acts as an axle which enables the tin wheels to turn when pushed.

String figures Mer Island, Torres Strait

A loop of string can be used to create string figures when put around and between the fingers in different ways. As in the European game of cat's cradle, string figures are often given names. This image shows three figures that children of Mer make.

The top figure is **king fish**; the bottom left figure is **bed**; the bottom right figure is **small fish**.

Girls telling stories in the sand
Ernabella, SA, 1995

Drawings made in the sand or earth may be used to show a range of information, from serious cultural lessons to simple fun stories.

They are found throughout Indigenous Australia and often go together with the telling of a story. Singing and gestures may also go along with the drawings. A favourite children's game is making imitations of the footprints of different animals and birds in the sand.

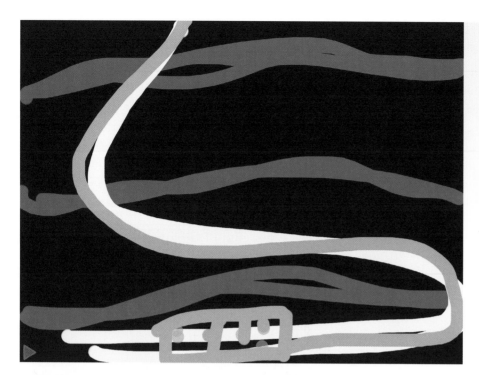

Telling a sand story with an iPad

Ngaanyatjarra Lands, WA, 2013

This image was created by Joella Butler on an iPad. She tells a story about going hunting through sandhill Country on the Ngaanyatjarra Lands in Western Australia.

🔊 **HOW DO YOU SAY IT?**

Ngaanyatjarra
ngah–nyuh–**chuh**–ruh

SERPENTS AND WALKING TRACKS

FINISH 36	35	34	33	32	31
25	26	27	28	29	30
24	23	22	21	20	19
13	14	15	16	17	18
12	11	10	9	8	7
START 1	2	3	4	5	6

©GM

Serpents and walking tracks

This game serpents and walking tracks is an Indigenous version of the game known as snakes and ladders. It was created by well-known Indigenous artist Gerald McGregor.

Language

A language is a tool for everyday communication as well as being a marker of a group's identity. In 1788, between 250 and 750 distinct languages were spoken around Australia. Only about 14 of these are still spoken by the children of the community on an everyday basis. Other languages are spoken only by the adults, and some haven't been spoken by anyone for a long time, but are being brought back into use.

The colonists placed great pressure on speakers of Indigenous languages to switch to English. They removed children from their families and forcibly moved speakers of different languages onto missions and reserves. There was often resistance, and people still managed to pass on parts of their languages to their children. But by 2016, 83.9 per cent of the 649 173 people who identified as Aboriginal or Torres Strait Islander in the census reported themselves as speaking only English at home. For more information on the forced removal of children from their families see Chapters 21 and 22.

Some non-Indigenous people (often missionaries) recorded language names, word lists, placenames, songs, stories and sometimes grammatical information about the languages they encountered. The first substantial record of an Indigenous language was of **Dharug** – the Sydney language. It was made by William Dawes, an officer of the First Fleet of 1787–1788. Few Europeans actually learned how to speak Indigenous languages. This was partly because the devastating effects of colonisation meant that, in many places, there were soon very few Indigenous people left to talk with, and partly because Indigenous languages are very different from European languages.

• • •

Mapping Indigenous social groupings across the whole country is a complicated task. The non-Indigenous researchers who first attempted this did not always agree on the correct way to show the different groups and the land on which they lived. One early attempt only placed group names on a map but showed no group boundaries. In 1974, Norman Tindale produced a very detailed map of group names surrounded by unbroken lines, which gave the impression that boundaries between groups were fixed. One useful feature of the AIATSIS Map of Indigenous Australia by David Horton (see over) is that the boundaries between the groups are blurred. This warns us that we should see these as approximate, rather than fixed, boundaries.

(see over)

WORD ALERT

mission

A mission is a community established by a Christian church group for Indigenous people to live in and provide them with education, including religious education.

reserve

A reserve is an area established by a government for Indigenous people to live in.

83

🔊 HOW DO YOU SAY IT?

Dharug
du-roog

FAST FACT

A young Dharug woman called Patyegarang taught Dawes the Sydney language.

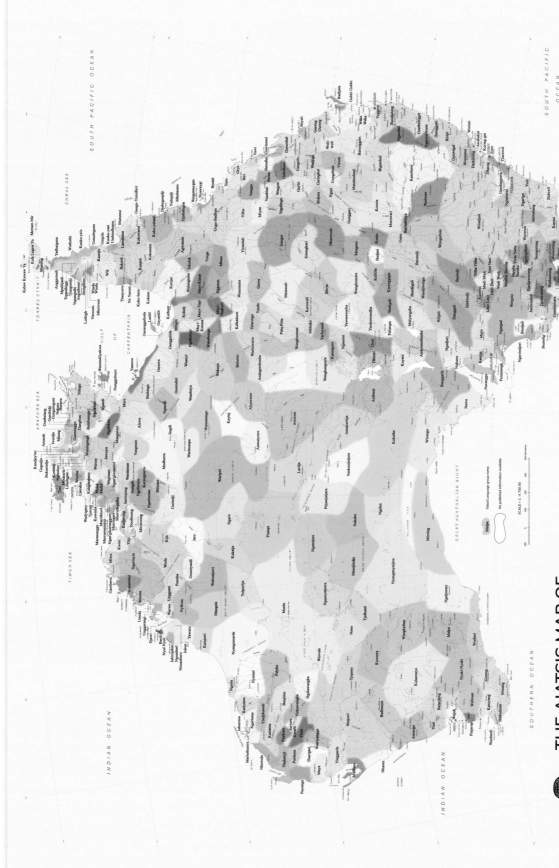

THE AIATSIS MAP OF
INDIGENOUS AUSTRALIA

David R Horton (creator), © AIATSIS, 1996. No reproduction without permission.

This map attempts to represent the language, social or nation groups of Indigenous Australia. It shows only the general locations of larger groupings of people which may include clans, dialects or individual languages in a group. It used published resources from the eighteenth century – 1994 and is not intended to be exact, nor the boundaries fixed. **It is not suitable for native title or other land claims.**

Speakers of Indigenous languages were not totally isolated from the influence of other languages. In the past few hundred years, the northern coast of Australia was visited regularly by people from Macassar and other islands of modern Indonesia.

Areas of genetic and language influence from outside contacts

As a result of the earlier visits of the Macassans, a significant number of people are of mixed Aboriginal and Indonesian descent on the islands and coasts of the Northern Territory 〰. On the Torres Strait Islands and Cape York there was contact between Papuan people, Torres Strait Islanders and Aboriginal people for several thousand years ▨.

Some coastal languages of the Northern Territory show traces of earlier visits by Macassans. Up to 300 words from the Macassan language were adopted into languages of this area.

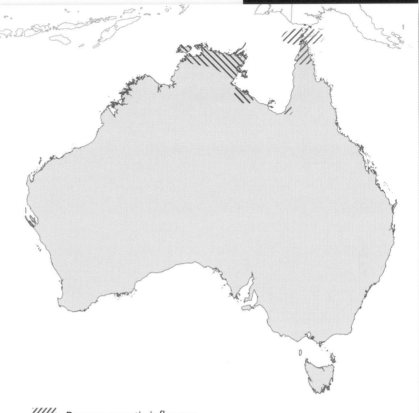

▨ Papuan genetic influence

〰 Macassan genetic and language influence

New words for new concepts

The flora and fauna of Australia and the culture of Indigenous Australians were completely foreign to the colonists. Some English speakers assumed there was only one Indigenous language, so they used the Indigenous language words that they knew as they moved further through the country. Indigenous people may have assumed that the word they were hearing was English and adopted it themselves to describe new items. A number of words from Indigenous languages entered English, mostly to describe things new to the colonists, such as:

- boomerang
- corroboree
- kangaroo

Some words for 'horse' in Indigenous languages

Horses were introduced by the colonists and so there was no name for them in Indigenous languages. People made up names from other things they knew about.

Nantu  comes from an Adelaide language where it meant a species of large kangaroo. It spread from Adelaide north to Darwin. *Yarraman* was first recorded around 1840, and most likely comes from a New South Wales language. It also found its way to north-east Arnhem Land. *Pangoonya* was used only in Tasmania. Other forms, including *timana*, *yawarta* and *ngort* were used in the languages over much of Western Australia.

\\\\ *Nantu*

//// *Yarraman*

\\\\ *Pangoonya*

//// Other forms (including *timana*, *yawarta* and *ngort*)

Some words for 'policeman' in Indigenous languages

Police had direct and regular contact with Indigenous people during colonisation. Words describing police were found in many Indigenous languages. One widespread form of naming relates the police to the act of tying up, grabbing, or using ropes ▢ . The idea of using a word for 'black cockatoo' ■ to talk about a policeman may have come from the colour of the police uniform. Using words for 'rock' and 'stone' ■ may be connected to money. Some languages call coins 'hard' like rock and stone. It may also be from the feeling that the policemen were 'hard' people.

■ Angry

■ Black cockatoo

■ Eagle, Hawk

■ Forbidden, Sacred

▢ Octopus

■ Prawn

▢ Rock, Stone

▢ Shark

▢ Sour, Bitter, Poison

▢ Tie, Grab, Rope

Speakers

The languages that can be considered strongest are those which have considerable numbers of adult speakers and are also spoken by the children of the community. This is true only in remote areas where few non-Indigenous people live, and Indigenous people form the majority of the population.

Percentage of people who speak an Indigenous language as a first language, 2016

Traditional Indigenous languages are still used in everyday communication in some of the remote parts of the Northern Territory, Western Australia, South Australia, northern Queensland and the Torres Strait. However, this is much less the case over much of the east of the country and the south-west of Western Australia.

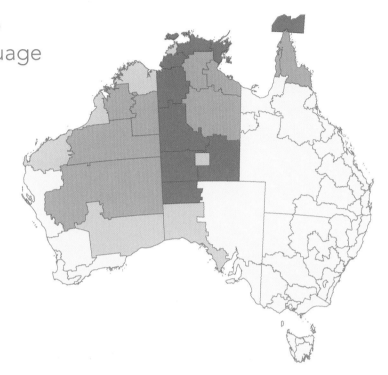

- Most 68.1 – 97.8%
- More 35.3 – 68.0%
- Less 7.9 – 35.2%
- Least 0.1 – 7.8%

Percentage of children aged 0–14 years who speak a traditional Indigenous language, 2016

One measure of whether a language is likely to survive is the number of children speaking that language as their main language. The pattern of this across the country is similar to the previous map, where children are most likely to speak an Indigenous language in some remote parts of the centre, the north and the west, but much less so in the east and south-west.

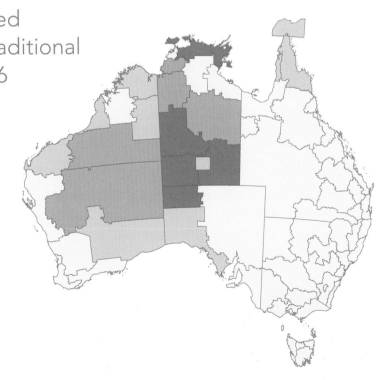

- Most 70.9 – 90.5%
- More 29.2 – 70.8%
- Less 5.8 – 29.1%
- Least 0.0 – 5.7%

Nine Indigenous languages with 1000 or more speakers, 2016

The nine languages with 1000 or more speakers are in the remote parts of the country, where most people are speaking a traditional language as their first language. These maps may suggest that living in remote areas can help languages to survive. However, another factor that may help language survival is the use of bilingual education programs, which recognise the importance of traditional languages by using them in schools. Eight of the nine languages on the map are in places with a long history of bilingual education.

In the Northern Territory, government schools ran bilingual education programs in which children were taught in their own language first, and then in English. In other states, independent schools had similar programs. Most bilingual education programs have now been discontinued, although the Northern Territory has reintroduced support for some programs. Funding has also been cut back for the vitally important work of maintaining, recording and relearning Indigenous languages. People who study languages also call Indigenous languages Australian languages.

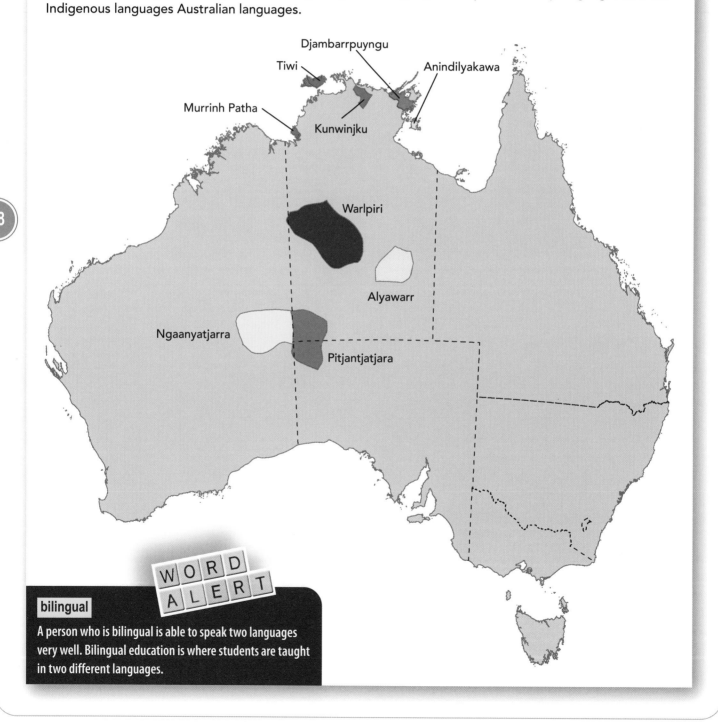

WORD ALERT

bilingual

A person who is bilingual is able to speak two languages very well. Bilingual education is where students are taught in two different languages.

As English-speaking colonists spread over the continent and attempted to communicate with local people, a new way of talking developed. A contact language is one which is formed between speakers of two completely different languages who find themselves in regular contact, such as through trade or colonisation. In these cases, the contact language usually starts out as what is called a 'pidgin' or, as with English colonists and Indigenous Australians, 'pidgin English' – a basic form of communication which mixed mainly English and the local Indigenous language. Over time, a pidgin can become the main language of a community, spoken as a first language from childhood. When this happens, the language is called a 'creole'. Contact languages are also called 'new' languages, as opposed to 'traditional' languages.

Contact language speakers, 2016

Two major creoles spoken in northern Australia are Kriol and Torres Strait Creole. Kriol is spoken across the cattle and sheep farming areas of the Northern Territory and the Kimberley. Torres Strait Creole is spoken in Torres Strait and along the north-east coast where many of the Islanders have moved.

- ○ 1–5 contact language speakers
- ○ 6–910 contact language speakers
- ○ 911–1960 contact language speakers
- ○ 1961–3700 contact language speakers

Speakers who have moved

Many Indigenous people have moved from remote locations to live in urban areas. For most of the languages that are still spoken as first languages, the majority of speakers are still found close to their traditional lands. There are some languages whose speakers have moved over a wider area.

Where speakers of Warlpiri are found, 2016

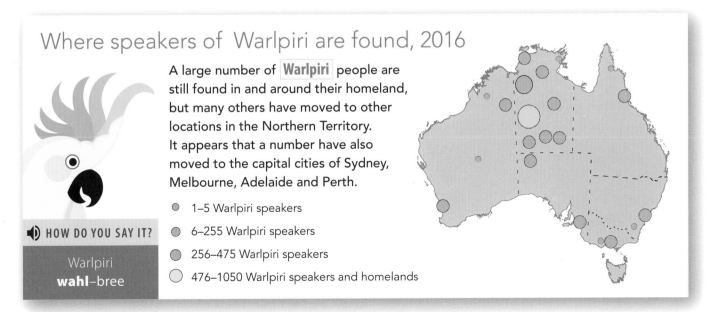

A large number of Warlpiri people are still found in and around their homeland, but many others have moved to other locations in the Northern Territory. It appears that a number have also moved to the capital cities of Sydney, Melbourne, Adelaide and Perth.

- ● 1–5 Warlpiri speakers
- ● 6–255 Warlpiri speakers
- ● 256–475 Warlpiri speakers
- ○ 476–1050 Warlpiri speakers and homelands

◀) HOW DO YOU SAY IT?

Warlpiri
wahl–bree

Where speakers of Pitjantjatjara are found, 2016

Many **Pitjantjatjara** speakers are also still found in and around their homeland. Some have moved to nearby locations in the Northern Territory, and others into parts of South Australia, south-east Western Australia and Victoria.

- ● 1–5 Pitjantjatjara speakers
- ● 6–195 Pitjantjatjara speakers
- ● 196–660 Pitjantjatjara speakers
- ○ 661–1470 Pitjantjatjara speakers and homelands

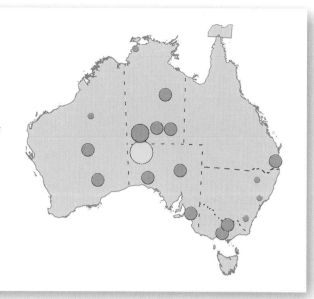

HOW DO YOU SAY IT?

Pitjantjatjara
pich–uhn–chuh–**chah**–ruh

Kalaw Lagaw Ya
kah–lah
lah–gow yah

Where speakers of Kalaw Lagaw Ya are found, 2016

The islands of Torres Strait are the heartland of the **Kalaw Lagaw Ya** language. The distribution of Kalaw Lagaw Ya on the map mirrors the known migration of Torres Strait Islanders from the Torres Strait to the eastern and coastal towns of Queensland. This reflects to some degree their preference for marine rather than inland locations and for moving within the state that they have a colonial history with.

- ● 1–5 Kalaw Lagaw Ya speakers
- ● 6–20 Kalaw Lagaw Ya speakers
- ● 21–200 Kalaw Lagaw Ya speakers
- ○ 201–560 Kalaw Lagaw Ya speakers and homelands

WORD ALERT

revive
If you revive something, you bring it back into use or practice.

Preserving language

There are now many language programs in place which are trying to revive languages which have fallen out of use or have very few speakers left. Historical records and documents, and knowledge of community members are used, although in some areas, very few records were made. There are also many language programs in place for languages still in use. Some languages – both still in use and revived – can now be studied as subjects at schools, colleges and universities.

Some institutions engaged in teaching, reviving and maintaining Indigenous languages, 2017

In the 1980s, the Australian government recognised the need to help Indigenous people to maintain or revive their traditional languages. A national program was set up and a network of language centres developed. This map shows the location of 22 language centres funded by the Federal Department of Communications and the Arts ●, and the location of universities teaching Indigenous languages ●.
The distribution of both kinds of institutions broadly follows the distribution of the Indigenous population and the urban centres.

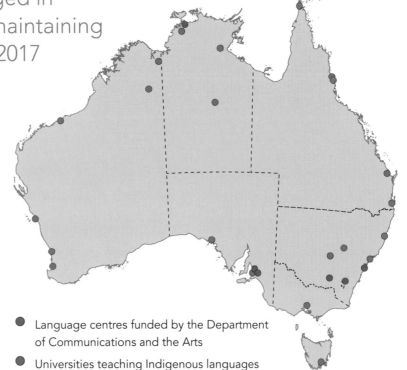

● Language centres funded by the Department of Communications and the Arts

● Universities teaching Indigenous languages

Location of languages that have substantial dictionaries

To revive Indigenous languages and support teaching programs, the languages need to be written. Language dictionaries are an important part of this task. The greatest number of languages with dictionaries are found in the Northern Territory and the north of Western Australia. This reflects the location of most language speakers, where most research has been carried out and reasonable records exist. Dictionaries of over 1000 words exist for about 50 languages. The largest dictionaries of Indigenous languages are for the Warlpiri and Eastern **Arrernte** languages in the Northern Territory.

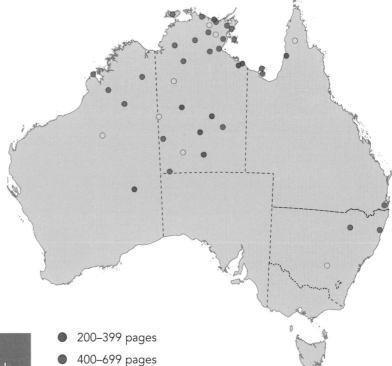

🔊 HOW DO YOU SAY IT?   Arrernte **ah**-ruhn-duh

● 200–399 pages
● 400–699 pages
○ 700 pages or more

CHAPTER 17

Placenames

This chapter looks at placenames in Australia which have Indigenous origins. There are thousands of places named using Indigenous placenames or other words. These range from towns to suburbs, streets, bores, dams and homesteads, and they represent an important aspect of Australia's identity as a nation. Naming can happen in a number of ways:

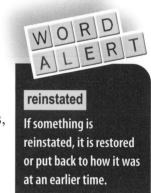

- Indigenous placenames may be given to previously unnamed places
- Indigenous placenames may be reinstated and replace non-Indigenous placenames
- Dual placenames may be established, where both an Indigenous and non-Indigenous name are used

Placenames are kept in records called gazetteers. There is a gazetteer for each state and territory and one for the whole of the country.

The gazetteers for Western Australia and South Australia show that around 50 per cent of the names of places in Western Australia, and around 30 per cent of those in South Australia come from Indigenous placenames or words. It is quite likely that the numbers are similar for all of the other states and territories in Australia.

🔊 HOW DO YOU SAY IT?

Yolngu
yool-ngooh

Bilingual road sign North-east Arnhem Land, NT

Indigenous words and placenames are often 'anglicised' which means they have been altered to sound or look more English. The road sign in this photo shows two spellings of the same name. DALIWOI BAY is the anglicised version and it applies to the whole bay. DALIWUY is the original **Yolngu** placename but it refers to just one place on the bay.

NOWRA Shoalhaven

Aboriginal for **Black Cockatoo**

🔊 HOW DO YOU SAY IT?

Pialligo
pee-**al**-uh-goh

Queanbeyan
kween-bee-uhn

The meaning of 'Nowra'

Shoalhaven City Council on the New South Wales South Coast has a practice of acknowledging the Aboriginal origin of names for townsites in its region. This photo shows that the town name of Nowra means 'black cockatoo'.

WORD ALERT

bore A bore is a deep hole made in the earth to reach an underground water supply.

soak A soak is a source of water which generally seeps into sand and is located underground.

Places named from Indigenous words, Western Australia

The gazetteer of Western Australia shows the kinds of places on the landscape that were named using Indigenous words.

This graph shows that over 50 per cent of all such places are associated with water – such as dams, bores, soaks and lakes. Water was an essential resource for both Indigenous people and the colonisers who would have relied on Indigenous people to help them locate the water sources.

Placenames of Indigenous origin in the Canberra region

Australia's capital was officially named Canberra in 1913. The name comes from a local Indigenous placename, whose likely form was Nganbirra. While the meaning of Nganbirra is not known, both 'meeting place' and 'breast' have been suggested. The road sign in this photo also features three other local placenames of Indigenous origin – Yass, **Pialligo** and **Queanbeyan**.

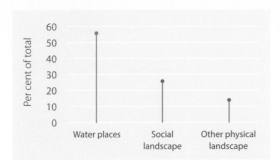

Per cent of total

60
50
40
30
20
10
0

Water places   Social landscape   Other physical landscape

Locations in South Australia

The distribution of locations with names taken from Indigenous words tends to be similar to the distribution of the general population. However, a number are also found in the area west of the Spencer Gulf and in the remote north-west where there are several Indigenous communities.

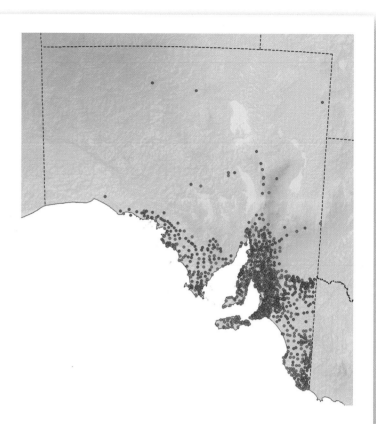

● Names derived from Aboriginal words

● Names not derived from Aboriginal words

Town sites in Western Australia

As in South Australia, the distribution of town sites named from Indigenous words is similar to the distribution of the general population. Town sites and people are mostly found in the southern part of the state – in particular, the south-west.

● Names derived from Aboriginal words

● Names not derived from Aboriginal words

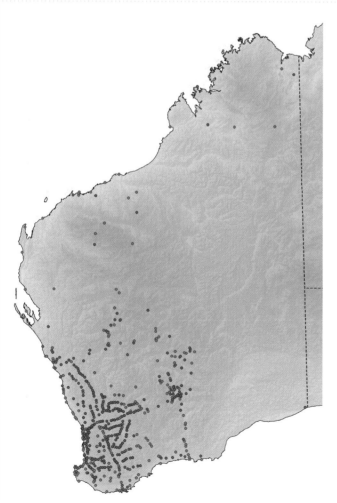

FAST FACT

All states and territories now have national parks with Indigenous names.

All states and the Northern Territory now have policies in place to reinstate Indigenous names or to establish dual placenames. Some examples of these include:

- River Torrens in South Australia is also called **Karrawirra Parri**
- Grampians National Park in Victoria is now officially Grampians Gariwerd National Park
- Mount Warning in New South Wales is also called Wollumbin

 HOW DO YOU SAY IT?

Karrawirra Parri
ku-ruh-wi-ruh pah-ree

Uluru NT

Uluru was named Ayers Rock in 1873 after the Premier of South Australia at that time. The rock, which is a sandstone monolith some 318 metres high, has deep spiritual significance for its Traditional Owners and iconic significance for all Australians.

It was returned to its Indigenous owners in 1985 and the name Uluru was reinstated to acknowledge Indigenous ownership. In 1993 the monolith was officially given the dual name Ayers Rock/Uluru. In 2002 the order of the dual names was reversed to Uluru/Ayers Rock.

 WORD ALERT

monolith
A monolith is a single, huge rock or stone.

Three placename endings

It is not surprising that Indigenous placenames are often connected to a particular thing or feature of the area. Also, placenames adapted from Indigenous words sometimes have endings that are taken from the language of the local Indigenous group and so are found over the territory or Country of that group.

This maps shows three example of these:

- Some languages of South Australia have names ending with **-awi**. Here, **-awi** means 'water' as part of the name for a water source, such as a waterhole, spring or soak. The official names of many water places have used this ending, but usually respelled as **-owie**. For example, Belcherowie Well between Adelaide and Lake Gregory is probably taken from the well's Indigenous name – Paltyarr'awi, meaning 'rat-water'.

- In Western Australia, the names ending **-ap** also means 'water'. It is part of the Noongar languages of the south-west. Officials have modified that ending to **-up** for many placenames in that region. For example, the town of Kojonup.

- In the Yolngu languages of north-east Arnhem Land, the ending **-buy** or **-wuy**, which means roughly 'place of', is a common ending of official placenames. For example, the mining town of Nhulunbuy, with the ending **-buy**, is named after a hill in that town. Earlier, official placenames had modified the endings of **-buy** and **-wuy** to **-boi** and **-woi**. The placenames with the endings **-boi** and **-woi** are shown on the map.

◀)) HOW DO YOU SAY IT?

Noongar
nyoong–ah

Nhulunbuy
noohl–uhn–boy

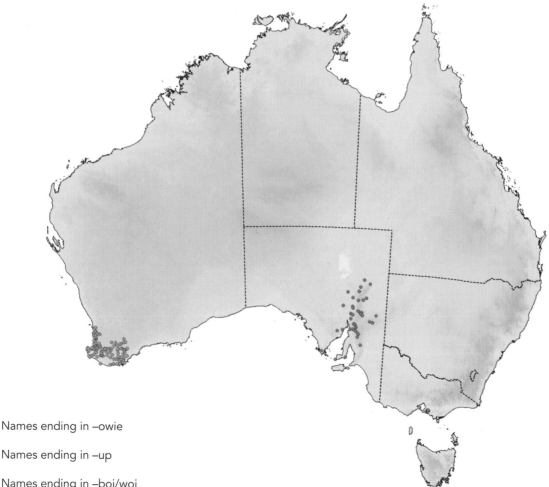

- Names ending in –owie
- Names ending in –up
- Names ending in –boi/woi

Land and water

This chapter looks at the Indigenous loss of rights to land and water caused by colonisation and the later return of some of those rights. The return of those rights has been uneven across the country. Most Indigenous-owned land is in remote areas where non-Indigenous occupation occurred late in the process of colonisation.

When the British began their colonisation of Australia, they treated the continent as if it were uninhabited, not belonging to Indigenous people and without any existing laws. They called this 'terra nullius' – the land of no-one. However, the Indigenous population already inhabited the entire continent and lived under their own laws in relationship to water, land, animals and other resources. Colonisation resulted in often violent conflict and the taking of land, waters and natural resources as the colonial frontier expanded. Returning these rights only began in the mid–1960s.

Occupation

The following three maps show how the colonial borders were changed with the spread of colonialism.

Indigenous occupation, pre-1788

In 1788, the Australian continent and its offshore islands were entirely occupied by Indigenous people and governed under their laws and customs.

Indigenous occupation

Non-Indigenous occupation, 1838

By 1838, colonial occupation of Australia was still limited to coastal regions, mainly in the south-east of the continent.

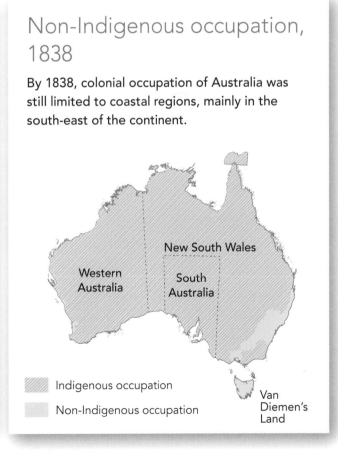

Indigenous occupation

Non-Indigenous occupation

Non-Indigenous occupation, 1888

By 1888, a century after the British occupation, much of the area suited to farming and running cattle or sheep had been taken over by the colonials.

Western Australia

South Australia

Queensland

New South Wales

Victoria

Tasmania

Indigenous occupation

Non-Indigenous occupation

WORD ALERT

unalienated Crown land

Unalienated Crown land is land which is owned by the state, which has never been given or leased to a person before.

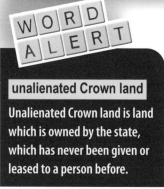

FAST FACT

The Mabo judgement was named after the late Eddie Koiki Mabo. He was a Torres Strait Islander from Mer Island who took the land claim for his community to the High Court and won.

Rights to land and water

The story of land return involves two separate notions – land rights and native title.

Land rights are special laws that governments have made to return some parcels of land to Indigenous people. In 1966, South Australia led the way in granting limited land rights under the *Aboriginal Land Trusts Act*. In 1976, the Commonwealth followed with the *Aboriginal Land Rights (Northern Territory) Act 1976* – ALRA for short – which returned all Aboriginal reserves in the Northern Territory to Aboriginal people. The ALRA also allowed people to claim unalienated Crown land.

Native title is the right to land and water by Indigenous people who have kept their connections to them. This came from the Mabo judgement, made in 1992 by the High Court of Australia, which said that colonial law had not destroyed the laws, customs and practices of the Meriam people of Mer Island in Torres Strait. Following this, the federal government passed the *Native Title Act* in 1993. This Act allowed Indigenous people across Australia to claim native title rights to land and waters. Many native title claims have been made. They are still being made and it is likely that the amount of land held by Indigenous people will increase.

Recording information on Country for a native title claim
East Arnhem Land, NT, 2000

This photo shows an anthropologist working with a senior clan leader and his son to record information about clan lands, place names and important sites in the claim area of Blue Mud Bay. The information and a comprehensive map were presented to the court in support of the case.

anthropologist

An anthropologist is someone who studies the beginnings and growth of humankind.

clan

A clan is a group of people who are related by descent from a common ancestor.

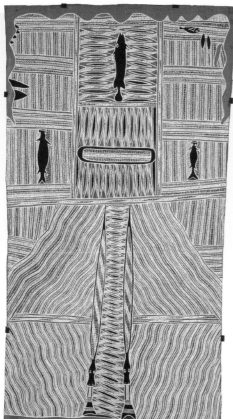

Djarrwark ga Dhalwangu Artist: Gawirrin Gumana, 1997

The late artist was involved in the original Blue Mud Bay Federal Court hearing, which concerned the land and waters of the Yolngu people of the region. He used this painting as evidence about ownership of the sea. It shows part of the land and sea Country of two Yolngu clans. The wavy line at the top represents the shape of the coastline. The major ancestral beings associated with the two sea Countries are shown in their animal forms. In the bottom half of the painting, the diagonal lines are the waters belonging to one clan. The vertical and horizontal lines are the waters belonging to the other.

🔊 HOW DO YOU SAY IT?

Yolngu
yool-ngooh

Djarrwark ga
Dhalwangu
jahr-wahk gah
dahl-wung-ooh

Indigenous-held land, 2018

By 2018, several forms of land rights and native title had given Indigenous people rights to approximately 47 per cent of the landmass. This map only shows the largest of these areas. The land shown as 'Indigenous-held' is simplified into the following three very broad types of possession:

The largest portion – 23 per cent – is held under non-exclusive native title. Non-exclusive possession means that native title holders can access land and waters for customary purposes such as hunting or performing ceremonies, but they have to share their Country with other individuals, government bodies or groups who have an interest in the land. This category is found in the remoter parts of several states and the Northern Territory.

12 per cent is held under exclusive native title. Exclusive native title is the legal recognition of the right to occupy and possess the land to the exclusion of all others. This land is mostly in Western Australia.

12 per cent is held under the various land right acts of other particular states. This land is mostly in the Northern Territory.

Smaller areas have also been returned to Traditional Owners in each state and territory. These smaller areas, including several in New South Wales, are not shown here.

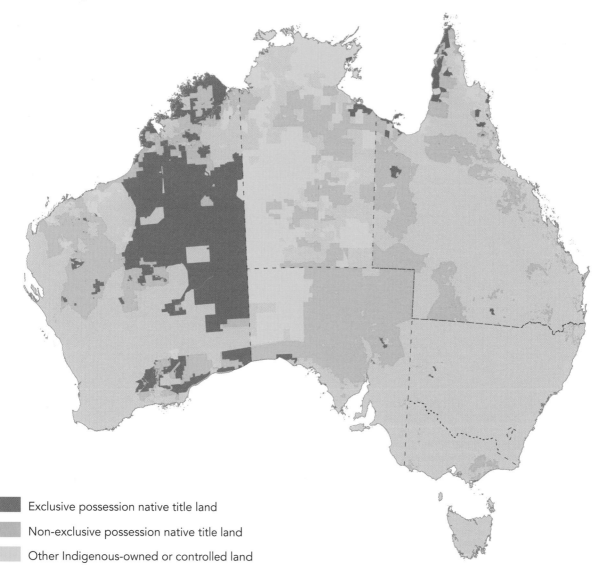

Exclusive possession native title land

Non-exclusive possession native title land

Other Indigenous-owned or controlled land

Ownership of the waters is as important as ownership of land for Indigenous people. Exclusive possession of sea waters cannot be claimed under native title but rights to occupy and use rivers may be granted exclusively over the land where native title has been granted.

Most native title judgements over the sea or ocean are non-exclusive. They usually include the rights for customary fishing and farming for personal use. Some native title judgements may include commercial rights to fish, others can extend to the intertidal zone. This allows Traditional Owners to control access to those parts of the water.

intertidal zone
The intertidal zone covers the area of water which sits between the high tide and low tide mark.

Indigenous marine rights, 2018

As of 2018, native title had been determined to exist ▬▬ over Torres Strait, portions of the coast of the Gulf of Carpentaria, the Kimberley, the Pilbara, the south coast of Western Australia, plus smaller sections of the east and south coasts. At that time, other parts of the coastal waters were under claim. Under the *Aboriginal Lands Rights Act 1976*, people have exclusive rights ▬▬ to the waters around the foreshore of a large part of the Northern Territory coast.

▬▬ Native title determined to exist

▬▬ Exclusive rights to intertidal zone
(*Aboriginal Land Rights Act 1976*)

Indigenous Land Use Agreements, 2018

An Indigenous Land Use Agreement is a voluntary agreement between Traditional Owners and individuals, organisations or governments about the use of land and water – ILUA for short. More than 1250 Indigenous Land Use Agreements have been registered so far. They range in size, and in total cover about 33 per cent of Australia's landmass.

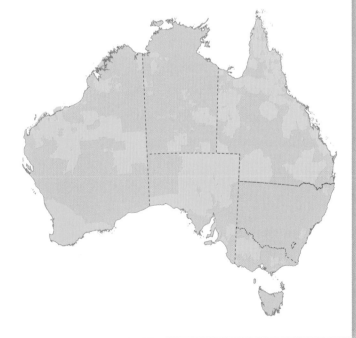

▮ Areas subject to Indigenous Land Use Agreements

Environment and Country

The word country can mean different things:

- an area of land with its own government and citizens
- land that is rural and away from towns and cities

The word Country with a capital C – as it is used in this Atlas – describes the traditional lands, waters and seas of Indigenous people. It is also commonly used in the phrase 'on Country' which means 'on one's traditional land'.

Environment

The Australian continent has a wide variety of climates. Despite this large variation, a large part of the continent beyond the coastal areas can be generally described as both hot and dry for much of the year.

Climatic regions

Australia is a vast continent, extending from the tropical north to the cool south.

The tropical wet |||||||| and monsoonal ⧄⧄ areas have a distinct dry winter season (the dry) and a rainy summer season with monsoonal downpours (the wet). Temperatures range from highs of 33°C in the dry to 40°C in the wet. The tropical or mid-latitude semi-arid ⧄⧄ and tropical or mid-latitude arid ⧄⧄ areas make up the very dry interior of the country. They include Australia's deserts and some of the farming country. The humid subtropical ⧄⧄, Mediterranean ⧄⧄ and maritime ⧄⧄ areas include the most productive land, the most comfortable climates and the highest populations.

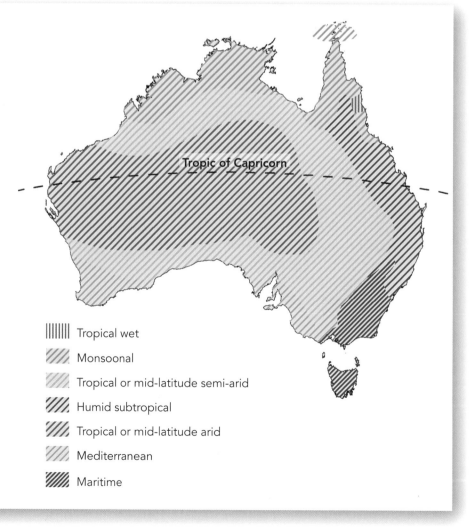

Tropic of Capricorn

|||||| Tropical wet

⧄⧄ Monsoonal

⧄⧄ Tropical or mid-latitude semi-arid

⧄⧄ Humid subtropical

⧄⧄ Tropical or mid-latitude arid

⧄⧄ Mediterranean

⧄⧄ Maritime

Indigenous land and vegetation condition

This map shows where the vegetation has been changed since colonisation. Where it has been changed least ▬ is also often Indigenous-held land. It has most of the original plant life and so has the potential for environmental conservation. However, the conservation value of Indigenous land is under threat from feral animals, invasive weeds, changed fire management practices, overgrazing, climate change and pollution from mining operations. The colours in the map key ▬ ▬ ▬ show how vegetation conditions have changed to varying degrees since 1788 within the 'least changed' to 'most changed' extremes.

WORD ALERT

feral
A feral animal is a wild or untamed animal.

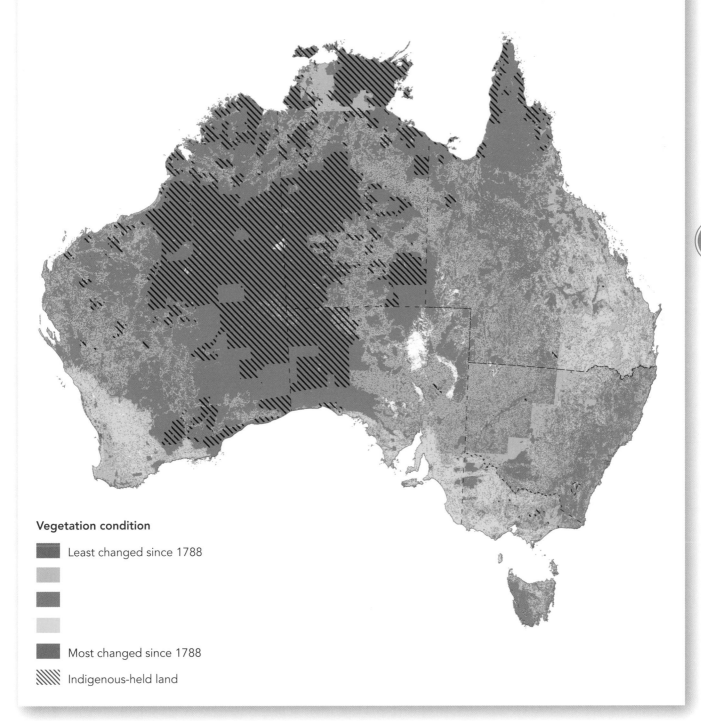

Vegetation condition

▬ Least changed since 1788

▬

▬

▬

▬ Most changed since 1788

▨ Indigenous-held land

Threats

Many new species of plants and animals have been introduced since 1788, some deliberately and others unintentionally. Feral populations of species such as buffalo, pigs, rabbits and cats cause environmental change and are often a threat to native flora and fauna. This is also true of introduced domesticated animals such as cattle, sheep and horses.

Threats also result from human activity, such as land clearing, practices of overgrazing, mining, weapons testing, pollution and climate change.

WORD ALERT

culled
If wild animals are culled, they are killed in an attempt to reduce the number of them.

Feral water buffalo
Photographer: Elizabeth McCudden, Arnhem Land, NT, 2015

Water buffalo from Asia were brought into the Northern Territory in the 1800s to supply meat to remote settlements. Feral buffalo spread over the wetlands of the north. They damage the ground and native flora which encourages the spread of weeds. They have been culled in Kakadu National Park but there are still large numbers further east in Arnhem Land. Many communities still hunt them for food.

The spread of the cane toad, 1935–2011

The cane toad was deliberately introduced in 1935 to control beetles in the Queensland cane fields. By 1974, it had spread to large areas of Queensland. Since then, it has moved to the top of the Northern Territory, the Kimberley region of Western Australia and the coast of New South Wales. It is poisonous to creatures that eat it, and so has had an impact on the populations of local fauna such as frogs, freshwater crocodiles, goannas, birds and small mammals.

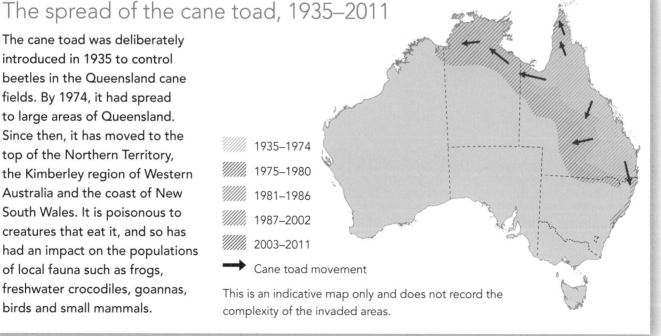

1935–1974
1975–1980
1981–1986
1987–2002
2003–2011

➤ Cane toad movement

This is an indicative map only and does not record the complexity of the invaded areas.

In the late 1940s, a rocket testing range was developed at Woomera in South Australia. Rockets were fired north-west across the desert to the Indian Ocean. The government considered the impact zone to be useless desert land, however, it crossed a large area of the Central Aboriginal Reserves where people lived. Patrol officers were sent to remove the people living on these reserves and relocate them to settlements – but not all were found.

A series of atomic bomb tests were carried out later, between 1953 and 1963, at Emu and Maralinga in South Australia, and on the Monte Bello Islands off the coast of Western Australia.

WORD ALERT

patrol officer

A patrol officer was an official whose job was to visit remote areas and report back on the conditions and needs of the Aboriginal people living there.

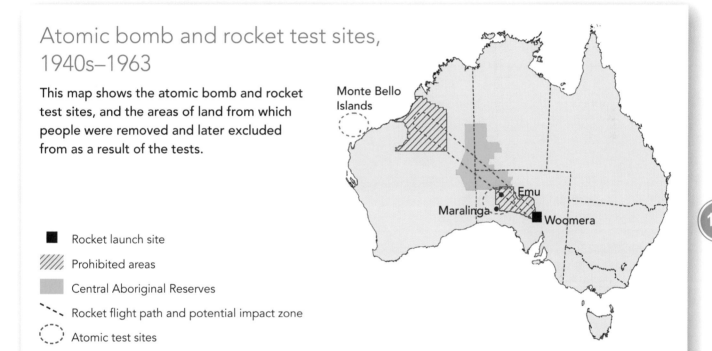

Atomic bomb and rocket test sites, 1940s–1963

This map shows the atomic bomb and rocket test sites, and the areas of land from which people were removed and later excluded from as a result of the tests.

- ■ Rocket launch site
- ▨ Prohibited areas
- ▨ Central Aboriginal Reserves
- - - - Rocket flight path and potential impact zone
- ⃝ Atomic test sites

Monte Bello Islands

Emu
Maralinga
Woomera

Mining and the extraction of oil and gas occur over large parts of the country where Indigenous people live or have land. These activities often damage the environment. Except in the Northern Territory, Indigenous landholders are largely unable to prevent mining on their Country.

Contamination sign Carpentaria Highway, NT, 2013
This sign warns of pollution that has destroyed local waterways. It is located downstream from a copper mine. Although the mine was closed in the mid-1990s, copper sulphide from the site continues to leak into a nearby creek.

CONTAMINATED WATER
NO DRINKING, SWIMMING
OR FISHING

Before colonisation, Indigenous people successfully adapted to changing climates and environment. However, those changes and their impacts were much more gradual than the changes that began with the development of industries in the modern economy. The world is warming up, causing an increase in extreme weather events and a rise in sea levels.

Projected rise in temperature extremes, 2081–2100

It is estimated if the present output of greenhouse gases is not reduced, sometime between 2081 and 2100 the whole country will be between 3°C and 5°C hotter. This will lead in turn to an increase in extreme weather events such as heatwaves, droughts, storms, cyclones and floods. These extreme weather events are more likely to occur in the central deserts and the north, where many small Indigenous communities are located.

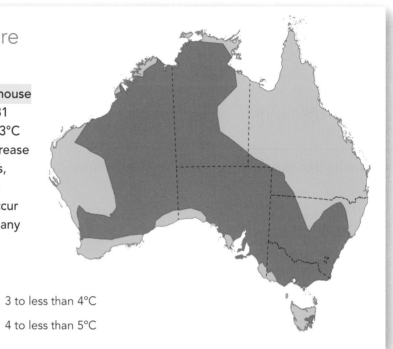

    3 to less than 4°C
    4 to less than 5°C

WORD ALERT

greenhouse gas

A greenhouse gas is a gas that contributes to the greenhouse effect. The greenhouse effect is when the weather gets hotter because the air all around the earth traps the heat from the sun, in the same way that the glass of a greenhouse does.

king tide

A king tide is a large rise and fall of the tide just after a new or full moon.

The oceans surrounding Australia have also warmed in the last century. Oceans expand as they warm, and the sea level rises. Rises in sea level increase erosion of coastal areas, especially during king tides and big storms.

Signs of coastal erosion
Torres Strait, 2007

Erosion caused by rising sea levels is a reality in Torres Strait where many islands are low-lying. The bottom right of this photo shows a graveyard being worn away by waves at high tides and during big storms.

Caring for Country

Indigenous people have always managed the environment by traditional burning practices and maintaining water quality. Some of Australia's most important conservation areas and tourist attractions are now owned and sometimes co-managed by Indigenous people. Indigenous Protected Areas – IPAs for short – are a special type of protected area. They are designed to encourage biodiversity and to support Indigenous people in the management of local resources. Each is managed under a voluntary agreement between a local Indigenous group and the relevant government agency. The first IPA was set up in 1998.

WORD ALERT

biodiversity

Biodiversity is the number and variety of different plant and animal life forms that live in an area.

Coming back to Country Far North Queensland, 2014

In Indigenous belief, people are part of their Country, and it knows them by their smell, which is also its smell. In many places, strangers, or those who have been away for a while, must be introduced to Country by having its smell put onto them, so that it will know and welcome them. This photo shows someone being welcomed back to Country.

People carry a heavy responsibility for keeping their Country, and everyone on it, safe. The increasing frequency and intensity of extreme weather events may make access to Country more dangerous and difficult.

Indigenous Protected Areas, 2017

Indigenous Protected Areas – IPAs – can be over large or small areas. The size and location of the IPAs appears to reflect the location and size of the areas of Indigenous-held land. The largest IPAs are mainly in the centre, north-west, and north of the country. The smaller IPAs are particularly common in the south-east where areas of Indigenous land are also smaller.

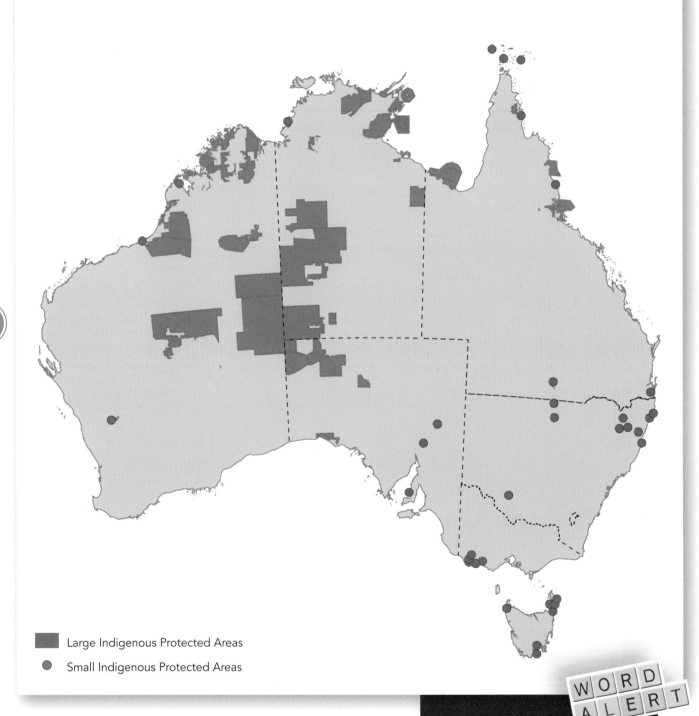

■ Large Indigenous Protected Areas

● Small Indigenous Protected Areas

WORD ALERT

ranger
A ranger is someone who looks after a national park or any other public area like this.

Location of ranger groups, 2017

Although a considerable number of ranger groups (22) are in the southern or non-remote parts of the country, the majority are found in the remote north where there are many Indigenous communities. This is probably because ranger groups are often organised by, and are part of, their communities where they are an important form of employment.

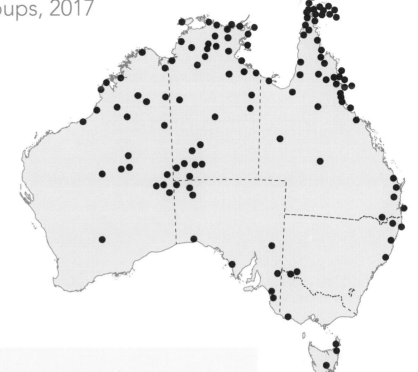

Planned firing Kakadu, NT, 1990

Traditional fire management is often called cultural burning or firestick farming. Fire was used to clear old growth and reduce the risk of extremely hot and destructive fires. Clearing the old growth encouraged new growth that attracted wild animals for hunting. Fires were often lit with a firestick – a smouldering stick which could be carried across distances. Ranger groups use fire management practices that are based on this traditional method. Firing of the land usually takes place in the cooler part of the year.

This photo shows a ranger firing land in Kakadu.

WORD ALERT 109

firing

Firing is the action of setting fire to something.

Colonialism and violence

Non-Indigenous exploration

Indigenous people often helped explorers – sometimes voluntarily – sometimes as captives. Their discomfort was noticeable when the expedition they were on took them too far from their home territory. Violence sometimes broke out between explorers and the inhabitants of the country they passed through, but it was in the explorers' interest to avoid conflict rather than to seek it.

The very earliest non-Indigenous explorations were by sea. Torres Strait was named after a Spanish explorer, Luis Váez de Torres, who sailed through the strait in 1606. The explorers of the 1600s made brief contact with Indigenous people, but it was not until the late 1700s that significant written records of these contacts began to be published.

The following six maps show the routes of the explorers as well as how the colonial borders were changed as the British government created new colonies.

Major non-Indigenous land explorers, 1813–1858

Contact with Aboriginal people was not the non-Indigenous land explorers' main goal. They were in search of land suitable for crops and livestock so as to feed a growing colony at Port Jackson in New South Wales. In 1813, a way was found across the Blue Mountains. Land suitable for the wool trade drew people to the west and Bathurst became a base for further exploration. In the 1820s and 1830s, the river systems of the south-east were mapped. By the 1840s the colonial explorers were venturing to the tropical interior and coasts.

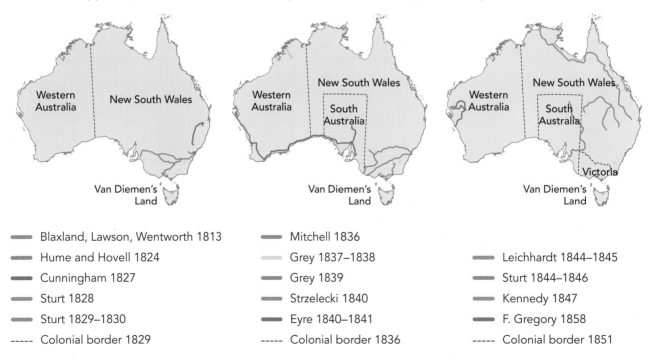

— Blaxland, Lawson, Wentworth 1813
— Hume and Hovell 1824
— Cunningham 1827
— Sturt 1828
— Sturt 1829–1830
----- Colonial border 1829

— Mitchell 1836
— Grey 1837–1838
— Grey 1839
— Strzelecki 1840
— Eyre 1840–1841
----- Colonial border 1836

— Leichhardt 1844–1845
— Sturt 1844–1846
— Kennedy 1847
— F. Gregory 1858
----- Colonial border 1851

Major non-Indigenous land explorers 1860–1910

From the 1860s, explorers ventured far into the interior. During the 1870s and 1880s, pastoralists followed them to northern South Australia, north-western New South Wales, Queensland and the Kimberley. In the desert areas, Giles, Warburton, John Forrest and Canning made their reputations for undertaking extremely long and difficult explorations. Over 1908–1910, Canning turned his exploration path into a stock route by making 52 wells. However, wherever the interior lacked reliable sources of water, Aboriginal people were left mostly undisturbed once the explorers had passed through their Country.

pastoralist

Pastoralism is the process of developing land for pasture for the grazing of animals, especially for meat or wool production. A person who does this is called a pastoralist.

stock route

A stock route is a path which has spaced sources of water, along which cattle and sheep can be moved.

Burke and Wills 1860–1861
Stuart 1860–1862
F. Gregory 1861
Jardine 1864–1865
----- Colonial border 1861

J. Forrest 1870
Warburton 1873
J. Forrest 1874
Giles 1875
----- Colonial border 1862–1863

Giles 1876
A. Forrest 1879
Canning 1906–1907
----- State/Territory border 1911

FAST FACT

Van Diemen's Land was the name originally given to Tasmania by the Dutch sea explorer Abel Tasman in 1642. It was named after the Governor-General of the Dutch East Indies (now called Indonesia). Van Diemen's Land was renamed Tasmania in 1855 after Abel Tasman. The Indigenous name for Tasmania is **lutruwita**. *You say it* **loo**-*troo-wee-tuh.*

Colonial violence

During the first 50 years of colonisation, the British government used troops in regions where Aboriginal people threatened the security of the colonists. Soldiers often arrested, killed or frightened Aboriginal people. Occasionally, Aboriginal people and soldiers fought battles.

Military operations against Aboriginal people, 1788–1842

The main military operations were in the south-east, where colonisation began and where the early colonists were afraid of losing their sources of food. In the 1820s–1840s, military activity spread with the expansion by the colonists into grassed and watered areas for pastoralism, and the Aboriginal people defended their land against the intruders.

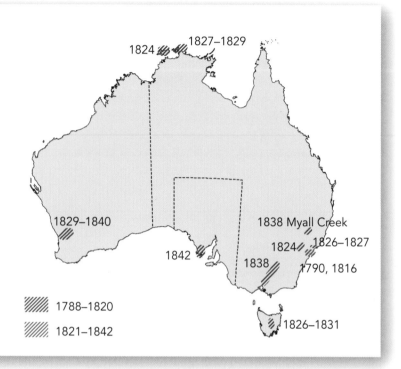

Frontier massacres in central and eastern Australia, 1795–1930

The term 'frontier massacre' is now used by historians to describe an attack where six or more undefended people were killed. This map covers only the eastern and central parts of the continent where research up until 2021 had discovered 250 instances of frontier massacres between 1795 and 1930. The map shows a significant concentration of these events in the south-east and in Tasmania. It is estimated that frontier massacres accounted for 80 per cent of Aboriginal deaths in Tasmania and around 60 per cent in Victoria. Overall, they may have resulted in more than 50 percent of the Aboriginal people being killed on the frontier across the whole continent. There are 10 known instances of Indigenous massacres of colonists between 1836 and 1900.

Indigenous attacks on European colonists, 1788–1932

This map shows some of the places where Indigenous Australians killed or harmed colonists and/or destroyed their property. Today, many Australians consider these incidents as 'Aboriginal resistance' to an invasion, but for most colonists at the time, they were seen as acts that deserved severe punishment and attack by colonists, soldiers and police.

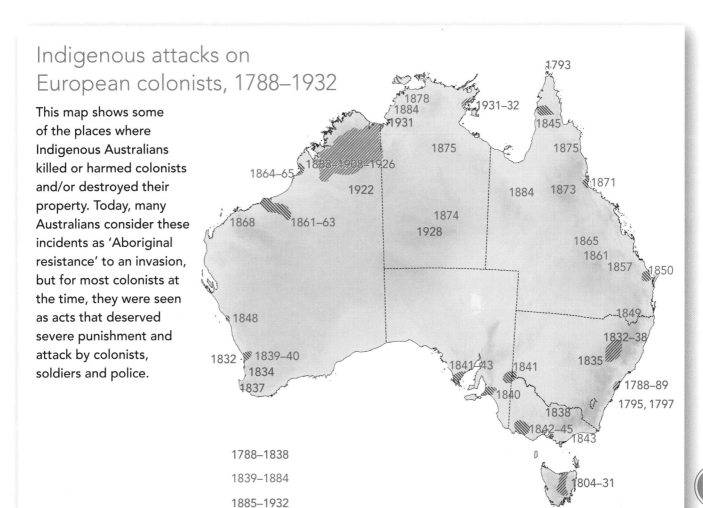

1793
1878
1884
1931
1931–32
1845
1875
1875
1864–65
1888–1908–1926
1922
1884
1873
1871
1874
1928
1868
1861–63
1865
1861
1857
1850
1848
1849
1832–38
1832
1839–40
1834
1837
1841–43
1841
1835
1840
1788–89
1795, 1797
1838
1842–45
1843
1804–31

1788–1838

1839–1884

1885–1932

Pastoralist and police violence against Aboriginal people

This map shows how pastoralism ▨ spread across the continent. Both pastoralists and Aboriginal people felt their livelihoods were threatened. When pastoralists introduced herds, they limited or prevented Aboriginal people's access to their plants, animals and water – their livelihood. When Aboriginal people first saw sheep and cattle, they hunted them as a new source of meat. The collision of these two cultures and ways of life resulted in violence.

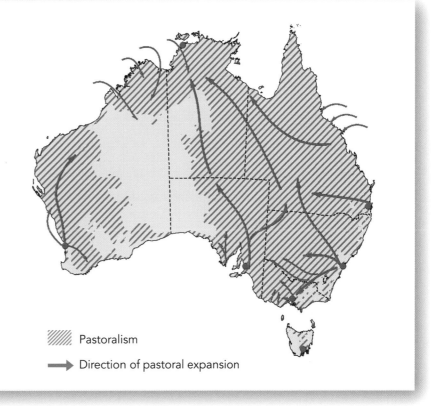

▨ Pastoralism

➡ Direction of pastoral expansion

The British government formed the first corps of Native Police in 1842, in what is now Victoria. The corps were made up of Aboriginal troopers and led by non-Indigenous officers. The official purpose of the corps was to limit violent clashes between the colonists and the Aboriginal people whose country the colonists were occupying. Aboriginal police were skilful in tracking, intimidating and, sometimes, killing Aboriginal people. They were often armed and rode horses. The corps were welcomed by colonists as long as they protected them and their herds from Aboriginal attacks.

Aboriginal groups had probably always fought one another – whether in formal battle, ritual combat or revenge attacks. However, disputes between groups were affected further by the colonial expansion.

In Queensland, the colonists were so fearful of Aboriginal people that they tolerated and even supported the physical violence often used by the Native Police. It is estimated that up to 40 000 Aboriginal people were killed by the Native Police there. The Native Police were disbanded just before 1914.

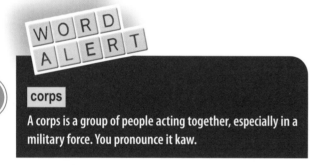

corps
A corps is a group of people acting together, especially in a military force. You pronounce it kaw.

CHAPTER 20

114

COLONIALISM AND VIOLENCE

The Native Police corps, 1842–1898

In the early period, the Native Police corps operated in the south and south-east of the country. Between 1861 and 1898, it was expanded into Queensland and some of the Northern Territory, wherever pastoralists felt threatened in their occupation of Aboriginal land. The corps was not introduced to Western Australia because that colonial government felt that its methods in other parts of the county were too violent.

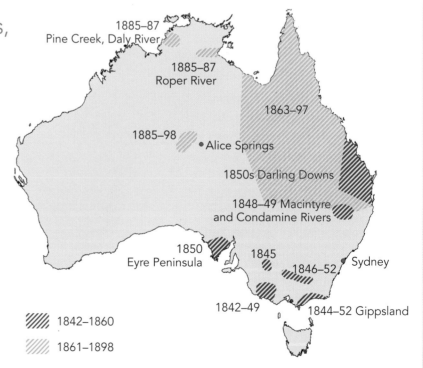

1885–87 Pine Creek, Daly River
1885–87 Roper River
1863–97
1885–98 Alice Springs
1850s Darling Downs
1848–49 Macintyre and Condamine Rivers
1850 Eyre Peninsula
1845
1846–52
Sydney
1842–49
1844–52 Gippsland

1842–1860
1861–1898

King plates

In 1817, the colonial authorities of New South Wales began awarding 'king plates' to Aboriginal people who they felt showed the qualities they hoped to find and encourage in the Indigenous population. Valued qualities included loyalty and usefulness to the British. These king plates were larger copies of the 'gorgets' worn by some British army officers in the 1700s. A gorget was a crescent-shaped badge which was worn around the neck as a sign of rank. However, unlike gorgets, some king plates had inscriptions such as 'King', 'Queen', 'Prince', 'Duke' or 'Chief'. As Aboriginal people became scarce in the settled districts, some king plates were also inscribed with 'the last of their tribe', though their descendants now say that they were not 'the last'.

King plate
North-east Qld, 1897

The king plate shown here was awarded to 'King Pepper of the Biria' in 1897.

Known distribution of king plates

The practice of awarding king plates ///// was confined mostly to the eastern parts of the country.

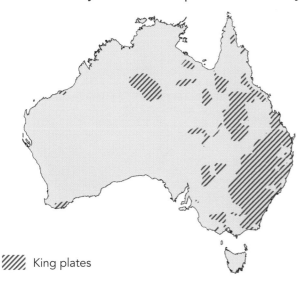

///// King plates

FAST FACT

The earliest gorgets were used in the days when soldiers wore armour. They were a piece of armour that protected the throat.

Two Australias

In 1970, Charles Rowley proposed that, for Aboriginal people, the colonial process had resulted in two different systems of authority – 'colonial' Australia and 'closely settled' Australia. The border separating these two systems is called 'Rowley's line'.

In the 'colonial' region – to the north and west of the line – the Aboriginal people remained relatively undisturbed and still lived according to their pre-colonial customs. There, a relatively small proportion of the Aboriginal population was of mixed Aboriginal and non-Aboriginal descent. White authorities, such as missionaries, pastoralists and government officials, were relatively powerful and backed by laws that, as late as the 1960s, restricted what Aboriginal people were allowed to do.

The 'closely settled' region – south and east of the line – included the capital cities and major towns. In this part of the country, Aboriginal people had interacted with non-Aboriginal people for a much longer time, including through marriage. The legal status of many of them was close to, or the same as, other Australians, although they still very much described themselves as Aboriginal. He explained the difference between the 'colonial' and the 'closely settled' regions by describing the different geography and impact of colonisation.

Rowley's line and remoteness

This map shows both Rowley's line and the areas of remoteness which were created by the Australian Bureau of Statistics in 2001. The degree of remoteness of a place was based on the distance it was from a range of services, goods, and opportunities for social interaction. The map shows that most of the region that Rowley described as 'colonial' is in what is now termed 'very remote'. Almost all of the region he described as 'closely settled' is outside the very remote parts and includes all of the capital cities and their surrounding areas.

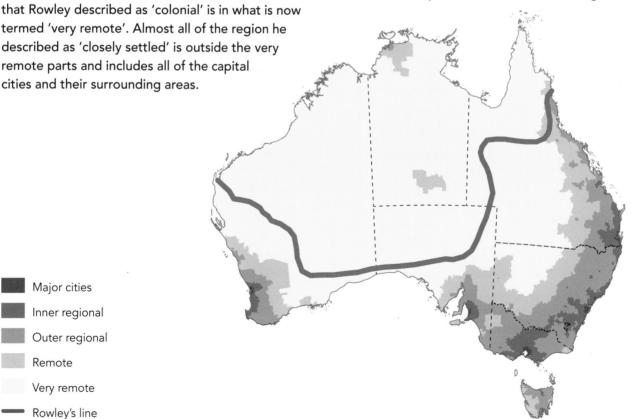

Major cities
Inner regional
Outer regional
Remote
Very remote
Rowley's line

CHAPTER 21

Social justice

The Stolen Generations

The practice of separating Indigenous children from their families goes back as early as 1814, when Governor Macquarie had children of mixed descent removed to a 'Native Institution' in Parramatta, New South Wales. Most removals occurred between 1920 and 1940, although they continued until the 1960s. Those affected are now often referred to as the 'Stolen Generations'. The practice and policy of removal occurred across the whole country.

An inquiry found that the official records of these events were inadequate and incomplete, and in some cases had been destroyed. It is thought that between 10 and 30 per cent of all Indigenous children nationally might have been removed.

FAST FACT

Indigenous children were sent against their will to government and church institutions, to various Indigenous communities, and to non-Indigenous foster families. These removals had damaging effects which are still being felt generations on.

117

People aged 15 years and over who said that they or a relative had been removed as children, 2014–2015

This map shows that between around 9 and 64 per cent of Indigenous individuals and their families have been affected by removal. The highest rates are in the west and southern parts of the country where many of the original Stolen Generation were relocated to.

- ■ Most 52.3 – 64.3%
- ■ More 37.6 – 52.2%
- ■ Less 16.0 – 37.5%
- ■ Least 8.8 – 15.9%
- ///, Interpret with care

Examples of the geographic distance people were removed

This map shows that children were sometimes moved very far from their homes. In one case, a child was moved from Darwin to Parramatta, west of Sydney. In another, girls were moved from Melville Island to Melbourne. In the third case, children were moved from Moola Bulla near Halls Creek to Perth. As well as the distress from being separated from their families, these moves would have led to the 'culture shock' that comes from being taken to a completely different cultural and physical environment.

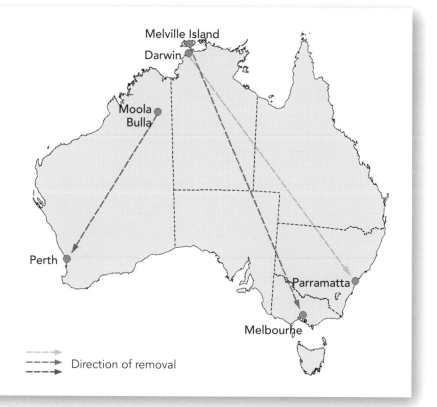

Direction of removal

She called him son Artist: Brenda L. Croft, 1998

Brenda Croft's father was a member of the Stolen Generations and first met his own mother just before she died. This image is based on the only family photograph of their reunion.

The Apology to Australian Indigenous Peoples

On 13 February 2008, the then Prime Minister Kevin Rudd made a formal apology to Australia's Indigenous peoples, in particular to the Stolen Generations. It was a moving occasion, with many Australians celebrating throughout the country. Here is the text of the Prime Minister's speech:

Mr Speaker, I move:

That today we honour the Indigenous peoples of this land, the oldest continuing cultures in human history.

We reflect on their past mistreatment.

We reflect in particular on the mistreatment of those who were Stolen Generations – this blemished chapter in our nation's history.

The time has now come for the nation to turn a new page in Australia's history by righting the wrongs of the past and so moving forward with confidence to the future.

We apologise for the laws and policies of successive Parliaments and governments that have inflicted profound grief, suffering and loss on these our fellow Australians.

We apologise especially for the removal of Aboriginal and Torres Strait Islander children from their families, their communities and their country.

For the pain, suffering and hurt of these Stolen Generations, their descendants and for their families left behind, we say sorry.

To the mothers and the fathers, the brothers and the sisters, for the breaking up of families and communities, we say sorry.

And for the indignity and degradation thus inflicted on a proud people and a proud culture, we say sorry.

We the Parliament of Australia respectfully request that this apology be received in the spirit in which it is offered as part of the healing of the nation.

For the future we take heart; resolving that this new page in the history of our great continent can now be written.

We today take this first step by acknowledging the past and laying claim to a future that embraces all Australians.

A future where this Parliament resolves that the injustices of the past must never, never happen again.

A future where we harness the determination of all Australians, Indigenous and non-Indigenous, to close the gap that lies between us in life expectancy, educational achievement and economic opportunity.

A future where we embrace the possibility of new solutions to enduring problems where old approaches have failed.

A future based on mutual respect, mutual resolve and mutual responsibility.

A future where all Australians, whatever their origins, are truly equal partners, with equal opportunities and with an equal stake in shaping the next chapter in the history of this great country, Australia.

Watching the Apology to the Stolen Generations Parliament House, Canberra, 13 February 2008
Members of the Stolen Generations and their families were invited to Parliament House in Canberra to witness the Apology. This photo shows Louise, Marjorie and Sylvia, who were part of the Stolen Generations, holding a photograph of their parents as Prime Minister Kevin Rudd delivers the Apology.

While an apology from the nation to the Stolen Generations was long overdue, it has not yet led to substantial improvements in social justice, or to any other social and economic results.

Criminal justice system

In 1997, the Human Rights and Equal Opportunities Commission suggested that the trauma associated with being removed as a child can have long-term effects. When the removed children grow up they are likely to suffer mental health problems and poor physical health, and to have their own children removed from them. More recent reports show that the forced removal of children also affects future generations, especially in connection to the justice system.

Indigenous people experience generally high rates of imprisonment. In 1994, in some areas of the country, more than one-quarter of the adult population had been arrested at some time in the previous five years. Indigenous people are much more likely to be arrested and imprisoned than non-Indigenous people.

Rate of imprisonment, 2017

Imprisonment rates vary significantly across the country. They are lowest in Tasmania and Victoria where the social and economic status of Indigenous people is fairly high. By far the highest imprisonment rates are in Western Australia, followed by the Northern Territory and South Australia. The rate of imprisonment in Western Australia is almost six times as high as in Tasmania.

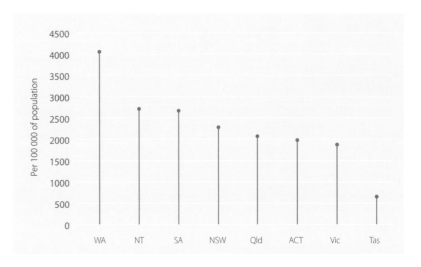

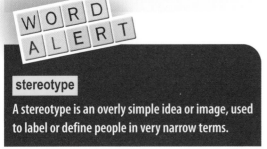

stereotype

A stereotype is an overly simple idea or image, used to label or define people in very narrow terms.

Indigenous people in Australia often experience discrimination because of widely held negative stereotypes among non-Indigenous Australians. Living with these experiences can have negative effects on health and wellbeing.

People aged 15 and over who said they experienced unfair treatment because they were Indigenous, 2014–2015

The proportion of people who feel they were treated unfairly because they are Indigenous can indicate 'discrimination'. People experienced the most discrimination in some southern parts of the country where they are a small proportion of the population. Discrimination tends to be lower in northern Australia, especially in the north of the Northern Territory and in Torres Strait. In these areas, Indigenous people are a larger proportion of the population. It may be that living in areas where a substantial number of people are Indigenous helps reduce discrimination.

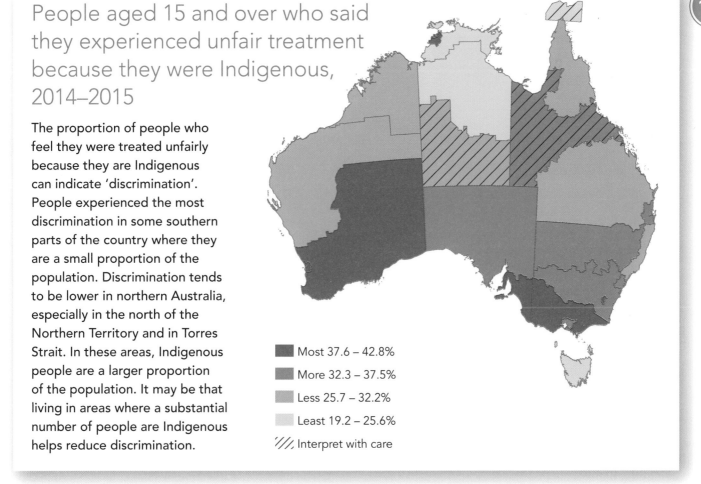

Most 37.6 – 42.8%

More 32.3 – 37.5%

Less 25.7 – 32.2%

Least 19.2 – 25.6%

////// Interpret with care

CHAPTER 22 Protest

A number of policies of 'protection' were introduced which caused great loss and damage to Indigenous people and their families and communities. They began in the 1800s and ran until the 1970s. Some of these policies included:

- the removal of Tasmanian Aboriginal people to Flinders Island
- the establishment of settlements for the Kulin people in Victoria
- laws which controlled where Indigenous people could live
- the requirement to live in supervised settlements
- the removal of people to institutions
- the separation of children from their parents

So called 'protections' such as these stripped Indigenous people of all of their rights. The pressure of this led to protests.

Protests, 1840–1946

Indigenous people objected to these policies of 'protection'. They demanded respect, land security, better employment conditions, and family life without interference.

This map shows places where people protested between 1840 and 1946. In some places, people wrote down their demands. In others, they simply removed themselves from a property, mission, or other place as an act of protest – a 'walk off'. Torres Strait Islanders protested against their pay and conditions in 1936 and stopped work on pearling boats. Station workers in the Pilbara region refused to work until employers increased their pay in 1946.

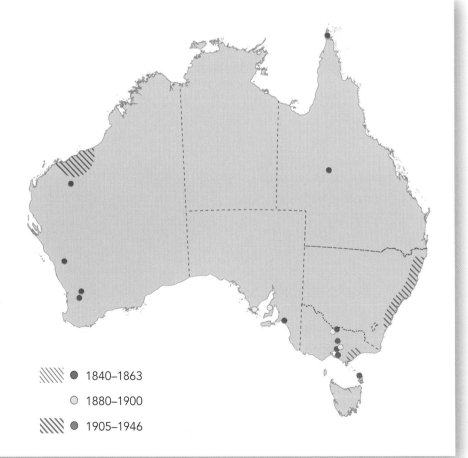

- 1840–1863
- 1880–1900
- 1905–1946

Robert Marbuk Tutawallie supports Aboriginal stockmen striking for equal pay at Wattie Creek
Artist: Robert Campbell Jr, 1990

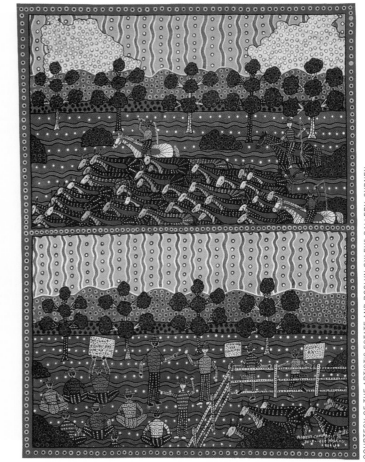

 In 1966, the stockmen and household workers of Wave Hill Station in the Northern Territory went on strike for better pay and working conditions. The strike was led by **Gurindji** elder Vincent Lingiari who was a stockman on the station. They walked off the station and set up camp about 30 kilometres away at a place called **Daguragu** – also known as Wattie Creek. In 1967, they sent a formal request to the Governor-General for their land to be returned to them. The strike lasted nine years until 1975 when the government funded their purchase of Daguragu. This was an important landmark in Indigenous land rights. There are now many Indigenous-owned stations.

The top panel of this artwork shows stockmen working with cattle. The bottom panel shows the stockmen outside of the station protesting.

123

🔊 HOW DO YOU SAY IT?

Gurindji
goo–rin–jee

Daguragu
du–goo–ru–gooh

Governor-General

The Governor-General is the main representative in Australia of the king or queen of the United Kingdom.

Charles Perkins and children in the town swimming pool
Moree, NSW, 1965

Charles Perkins was one of the Freedom Riders protesting against the policies of discrimination and segregation relating to Indigenous people. The public swimming pool in Moree did not permit entry to Aboriginal people. This photo shows Aboriginal activist Charles Perkins with a group of local Aboriginal children defying the exclusion ban.

The route of the Freedom Ride
12–26 February, 1965

In 1965, young white activists joined with Aboriginal activists in what became known as the 'Freedom Ride'. Two years before, the New South Wales government had put an end to laws discriminating against Aboriginal people, but practices of racial segregation had remained in some towns. The Freedom Riders' visits to these towns challenged the residents to admit Aboriginal people to public spaces such as swimming pools and cinemas. The press in the cities reported the Freedom Ride sympathetically.

This map shows the towns where the Freedom Riders demonstrated, where they stopped overnight, and other places they visited on the route. The Freedom Ride started and ended in Sydney and took fourteen days.

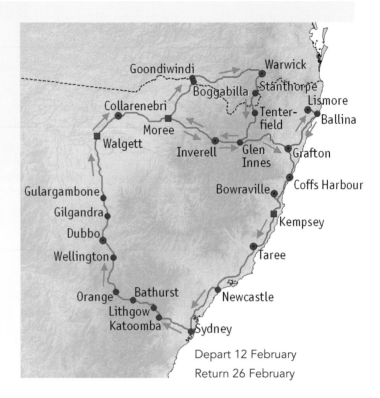

Depart 12 February
Return 26 February

● Overnight stop
■ Overnight stop and demonstration
● Other places visited
→ Direction travelled

FAST FACT

In 1969 and 1973, the New South Wales government passed the Aborigines Act to give Aboriginal people some voice in future discussions of their welfare.

WORD ALERT

activist

An activist is someone who works very hard for something they believe in, especially a political cause.

racial segregation

Racial segregation is the enforced separation of different racial groups living in the same country or area. Separate schools, hospitals, and other facilities may be provided, or access to facilities may be restricted or denied for a specific racial group.

26 January was named 'Australia Day' to commemorate the anniversary of the landing of Governor Phillip at Sydney Cove in 1788, which began British settlement in Australia. Celebration of this date continues the colonial view that Australian history basically started from this point in time.

Indigenous people have staged events on 26 January to rename this day as 'Survival Day' or 'Invasion Day'. For Indigenous people and their supporters it is a commemoration of the impact that the arrival of the Europeans has had on Indigenous people, and their language and culture. There have been calls to 'change the date' for many years now.

Change the date

This poster was published in *The Saturday Paper* on 23 December, 2017. The image portrays Captain James Cook not as the 'discoverer' of Australia, but as being thrown out of the biblical Garden of Eden for committing a sin. The text calls to 'change the date' that Australia Day is commemorated.

January 26 is not a holiday.

Ask to work.

Change the Date

Don't celebrate dispossession.

Daniel Boyd, *Fall and Expulsion* (detail), 2006

This is a call to work. As long as politicians ignore the need to move Australia Day, you should ignore it. Don't celebrate a day that continues the hurt of Australia's First Peoples.

If you own a business, ask your staff to work. If you're an employee, ask to work and take a day in lieu. We need a new Australia Day for all Australians. Saying no to this one is the only way we'll get it.

changedate.com.au

SATURDAY PAPER

Black Lives Matter protest

Parliament House, Canberra, 5 June 2020

There is now an international movement which is seeking to raise awareness of systemic racism and violence against black people and to eradicate it. The 'Black Lives Matter' movement was founded in the US in response to the treatment of African Americans. This movement expanded to different countries and to different racial groups. In Australia, it has highlighted the discrimination, racism, violence and injustice long experienced by Indigenous Australians. Both Indigenous and non-Indigenous Australians have joined demonstrations and protest marches to push for change. This photo shows protesters outside of Parliament House in Canberra.

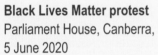

Symbols of nationhood

This chapter looks at some of the symbols of nationhood for Indigenous Australians.

The Aboriginal flag

The Aboriginal flag was designed in 1971 by a Luritja man, Harold Thomas.

- the black represents the people
- the red represents the earth and the people's relationship to it
- the yellow represents the sun

The flag was first flown in Adelaide's Victoria Square in 1971, and became known nationally when it was flown at the Tent Embassy in 1972.

The Torres Strait Islander flag

The Torres Strait flag was designed in 1992 by Thursday Island school student, the late Bernard Namok.

- the black represents the people
- the green represents the land
- the blue represents the sea
- the five-pointed star represents the island groups
- the white symbol which sits over the star is a 'Dari' – a traditional headdress.

Aboriginal Tent Embassy, 1972

The Aboriginal Tent Embassy was established on the lawns outside Parliament House on Australia Day, 26 January 1972, in protest of the government's refusal to acknowledge Indigenous land rights. The police tried to forcefully remove it a number of times, but it remained until February 1975, when Charles Perkins and the Minister for the Australian Capital Territory negotiated its peaceful removal.

Aboriginal Tent Embassy
2018

On Australia Day (or Survival Day or Invasion Day) 1992, the Aboriginal Embassy was re-established on the lawns outside what was by then Old Parliament House. It remains there to this day as a constant presence.

W O R D
A L E R T

Australian Constitution

A constitution is a set of basic rules for governing a state, society, or other organisation. The Australian Constitution outlines the structure, laws and powers of Australia's government. The constitution may only be changed through a vote by the Australian public through what is called a referendum.

🔊 HOW DO YOU SAY IT?

Makarrata
mah–kuh–**rah**–tuh

Yolngu
yool–ngooh

127

In recent years, there has been growing public debate about the need for recognition of Aboriginal and Torres Strait Islander peoples in the Australian Constitution. In May 2017, the First Nations National Constitution Convention took a significant step in issuing the Uluru Statement from the Heart. Here are parts of the Statement:

> **Makarrata** is the culmination of our agenda: the coming together after a struggle. It captures our aspirations for a fair and truthful relationship with the people of Australia and a better future for our children based on justice and self-determination. We seek a Makarrata Commission to supervise a process of agreement-making between governments and First Nations and truth-telling about our history.
>
> We invite you to walk with us in a movement of the Australian people for a better future.

The term Makarrata comes from the **Yolngu** languages of north-east Arnhem Land. It is the name for a form of ceremony used to settle disputes and make peace. The Uluru Statement represents a generous reaching out of Indigenous peoples to other Australians. It advocates a path to a reconciliation based on truth and social justice.

The Uluru Statement from the Heart, 2017

The Uluru Statement calls for:

- the establishment of a First Nations Voice included in the Australian Constitution
- a Makarrata Commission to supervise agreement-making between governments and First Nations
- truth-telling about Australian history

The government rejected these calls in late 2017, but important Indigenous figures have continued to promote the Uluru Statement as the way forward.

FAST FACT

The term 'First Nations' was used in the Uluru Statement from the Heart, reflecting a renewed desire by Indigenous people for them to be referred to in this way.

Makarrata: Voice Truth Treaty
25 August, 2017

This photo shows Gurindji people commemorating the 50th anniversary of the Wave Hill walk off. The people are voicing their support for the Uluru Statement and marching behind a banner that captures its message. More information on the Wave Hill walk off can be found in Chapter 22.

Welcome to Country and Acknowledgement of Country

A **Welcome to Country** is a welcome given by someone, such as an Aboriginal Elder, who is a representative of the traditional Indigenous custodians of the land on which the event is taking place. The welcome may be a speech only or it may include a performance. This depends on the region where the welcome is taking place.

🔊 HOW DO YOU SAY IT?

Gurindji
goo–rin–jee

An **Acknowledgement of Country** is an official recognition of the Indigenous Traditional Custodians of a locality and can be performed by either a non-Indigenous or an Indigenous person.

The wording may be different in different places, but here are two examples of what is commonly said in an Acknowledgement of Country:

I would like to begin by acknowledging the Traditional Custodians of the land on which we gather today, and pay my respects to their Elders past and present. I extend that respect to Aboriginal and Torres Strait Islander peoples here today.

I would like to begin by acknowledging the (_____) people, Traditional Custodians of the land on which we gather today, and pay my respects to their Elders past and present. I extend that respect to Aboriginal and Torres Strait Islander peoples here today.

(The name of the people who are the recognised Traditional Custodians would be filled in.)

Population and residence

In 2016, the Indigenous population was 649 173 – around 3 per cent of the Australian population. This was made up of 590 062 people who said they were Aboriginal, 32 344 who said they were Torres Strait Islanders, and 26 767 who said they wanted to be known as both.

Population decline and growth, 1788–2016

The estimated population at colonisation in 1788 was 500 000. By around 1933, the population had been reduced – by introduced diseases, lower fertility rates and violence – to approximately 20 per cent of the size before colonisation. The 1950s saw the population increasing. Since the 1970s, the numbers have risen steeply and now go beyond the original population of 500 000. This increase is the result of:

- improved health conditions
- a rise in fertility
- people being officially counted as Indigenous since the 1971 Census
- more people choosing to identify as Indigenous

The figures shown in this graph are estimates up until the 1970s, after this they are census data.

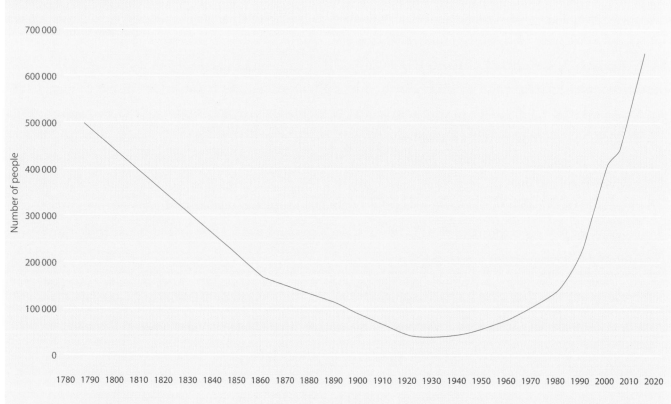

Over the past 200 years, there has been a gradual shift in the distribution of the population from remote and rural areas to urban centres. The trend began as a result of government policies of forced removal and the dispossession of lands.

Remote areas, 2016

In 2001, the Australian Bureau of Statistics came up with a way of measuring the 'remoteness' of a place. The degree of remoteness of a place was based on the distance it was from a range of services, goods, and opportunities for social interaction. In 2001, about 25 per cent of all Indigenous people lived in remote and the very remote regions. Since then, with a rise in urban living, this figure has slowly decreased to around 20 per cent.

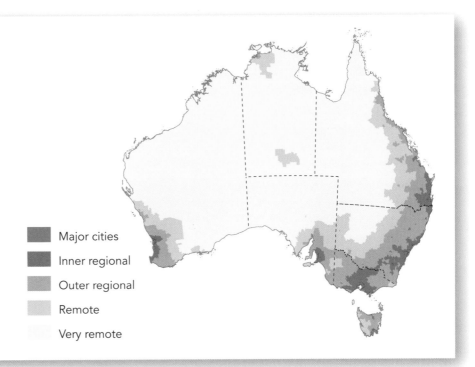

Major cities
Inner regional
Outer regional
Remote
Very remote

131

Distribution of the Indigenous population, 2016

The current distribution of the Indigenous population shown in this map follows that of the total Australian population – with the largest numbers along the highly populated east coast, in major towns and in capital cities. These are the parts of the country that are richest in natural resources and are where researchers estimate most Indigenous people would also have lived before Europeans arrived.

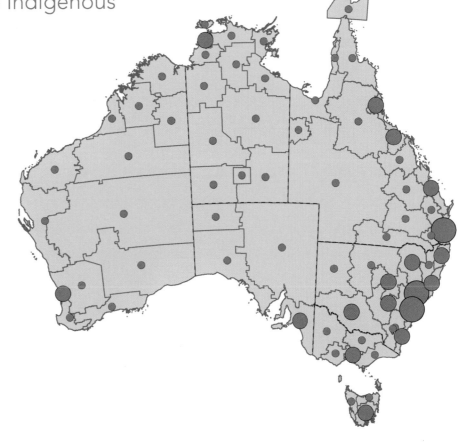

Population

● 1000 – 10 000

● 10 001 – 32 000

● 32 001 – 72 000

The Indigenous population as a percentage of the total population, 2016

Indigenous people make up the majority of the population in many of the remotest areas. You can see on the map that these areas include Torres Strait through to the desert regions of Western Australia. This is especially the case in areas distant from the larger towns and service centres. For example, in parts of Arnhem Land, around 90 per cent of the total population is Indigenous. In other parts of the country, such as the south and the east of the country, they are a very small percentage of each area.

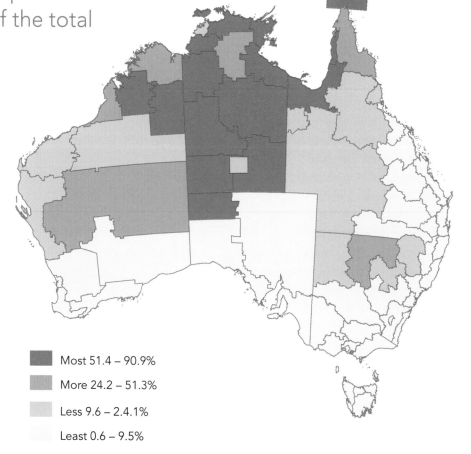

Most 51.4 – 90.9%

More 24.2 – 51.3%

Less 9.6 – 2.4.1%

Least 0.6 – 9.5%

The previous two maps reveal an important feature of the Indigenous population distribution. Most Indigenous people live in the most populated areas where they are just a very small proportion of the total – becoming almost invisible. And, a much smaller number of them live in the less populated parts where they can be a large proportion of the total – and extremely visible.

FAST FACT

Until the end of World War II, most Torres Strait Islanders were confined by law to the islands of Torres Strait. When the restrictions on movement were lifted, Islanders began to travel to the mainland in search of employment and services. Now nearly 90 per cent live outside Torres Strait – with most in the urban centres along the coast of Qld and NSW.

Distribution of Indigenous communities, 2006

Many of today's communities – in urban settings as well as in remote and rural areas – were formerly:

- mission stations
- government settlements or reserves
- areas cut from large cattle stations and farms
- special-purpose leases within towns

This map shows that most of the smaller of these communities are in the remote centre and north of the country. Their location and distribution reflects the periods of dispossession and the giving back of property or rights described in Chapter 18. Many of these communities are now on legally recognised Indigenous land, or land that is being claimed under native title.

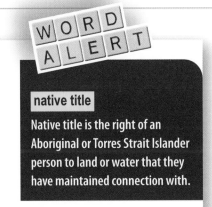

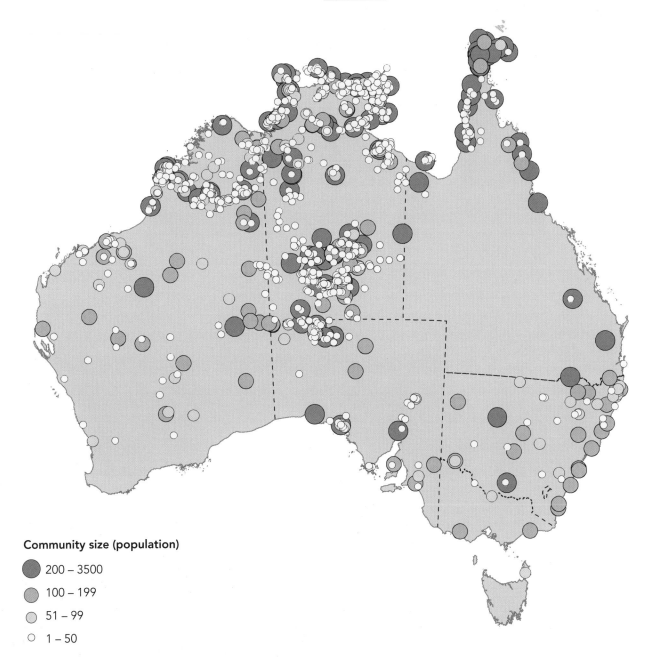

Community size (population)

- 200 – 3500
- 100 – 199
- 51 – 99
- 1 – 50

Community housing Adelaide Bore, NT, 2005

Indigenous community housing programs of the 1970s often provided basic shelters in remote areas. By the 1990s, most community dwellings were more substantial and conventional, like the middle dwelling of the three in this photo.

La Perouse street view La Perouse, NSW, 1988

This photo shows urban dwellings in the suburb of La Perouse. In 1881, a group of Aboriginal people from the Sydney, Botany Bay and Wollongong areas established a permanent camp at La Perouse. This was 15 kilometres from what is now Sydney's business district. The United Aborigines Mission based themselves there in 1894, and it became a reserve the following year. The population grew steadily with people who had been dispossessed by extensive farming and timber felling in the south. La Perouse remains an area with a relatively high Indigenous population.

CHAPTER 25

Education

Indigenous Australians have taught their children skills and knowledge for thousands of years. Children first learnt about their Country, kinship and the spiritual world through informal instruction and observation. Older children were taught about the rites and ceremonies that would be needed as part of the process of becoming an adult. These forms of education are still carried out today.

Learning bark painting
North-east Arnhem Land, NT, 1971

This photo shows the late artist Narritjin Maymuru working with his son Mowandi on a bark painting. The boy is learning through first watching his father and then following his instructions to apply a layer of ochre to the surface.

The importance of language and culture to learning has always been recognised by Indigenous people. They have aimed to find ways that Western schooling complements their traditional approaches to education rather than smothering them.

Bilingual programs were first introduced in the 1960s and 1970s in some schools in Western Australia, the Northern Territory, South Australia and Queensland for Indigenous children who did not speak English as their first language. In most bilingual schools children were taught mainly in their own language in the early years. This was followed by a gradual transfer to English in the later years of primary school.

◄》 HOW DO YOU SAY IT?

Alyawarr
uhl–**yah**–wah–ruh

Anmatyerre
uhn–**mah**–juh–ruh

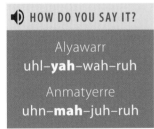

Arlparra School Family Learning Centre students
Utopia, NT, 2018

The Arlparra Family Learning Centre is located in Utopia, 250 kilometres north-east of Alice Springs. The Learning Centre is part of the Arlparra school and provides early childhood education for Alyawarr and Anmatyerre speaking preschoolers. The Learning Centre also provides a mobile outreach program to the area's more remote communities.

Another approach to learning that is becoming more widespread is called 'Learning on Country'. In these programs young people who are enrolled in school spend time with elders and Indigenous rangers on Country. Here, traditional Indigenous knowledge is shared and then used to complement Western knowledge. In this way, learning is enriched and both systems of knowledge valued.

Young people on a remote field trip
West Kimberley, WA, around 1982

Starting around the mid-1970s, researchers working on Indigenous land rights and site protection issues often had access to four-wheel drives. This allowed them to take people to visit remote places they had left, or been removed from, years earlier. Younger family members would be included in these field trips, giving them firsthand knowledge of their Country. This photo shows Wayne and Anthony Watson with a researcher on one of these trips. Anthony Watson later became the chairman of the Kimberley Land Council.

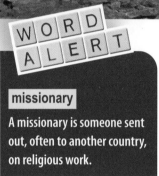

WORD ALERT

missionary
A missionary is someone sent out, often to another country, on religious work.

Western education was first introduced in many places by missionaries. They came to 'save souls' by converting Indigenous people to Christianity and to replace their traditional ways of life with Western practices. By establishing schools, the missionaries hoped the children would take the Western practices they had been taught home and share them with their families and communities.

Indigenous people are increasing their participation in education and training over time, but they still fall behind other Australians. Across the country preschool attendance rates are nearly the same as for other Australians, but secondary education and tertiary education rates are lower. They are particularly lower in remote areas. There is a growing divide between remote areas and the rest of the country which is concerning.

Boarding schools attended by Indigenous students, 2018

Many Indigenous students living in remote areas don't have access to secondary education within their communities. For a number of years now, boarding schools have been an option for many of these students. You can see from the map that the boarding schools are mainly in the more urbanised parts of the country.

In 2018, there were well over 3000 Indigenous students attending nearly 190 boarding schools across Australia. The number of Indigenous boarders is rising and this shows how necessary and important the option of boarding schools are for families and communities in remote areas.

Children aged 5–17 attending school, 2016

Three of the maps in this chapter use the comparisons of Most ■ , More ■ , Less ■ , and Least ■ . A percentage range is given for each category. This map shows that attendance is highest in the urban and some regional areas and lowest in the remote desert and Top End communities.

Attendance in the early years of primary school is quite high but it starts to drop as students reach the upper primary and early high school years.

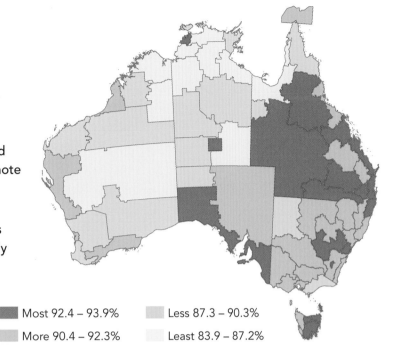

■ Most 92.4 – 93.9%   ■ Less 87.3 – 90.3%
■ More 90.4 – 92.3%   ■ Least 83.9 – 87.2%

WORD ALERT

Top End

The Top End is another name for the northern part of the NT.

boarding school

A boarding school is a type of school where students live and are provided with meals.

Tertiary education is any form of education beyond the school system, such as technical colleges and universities. Courses vary widely in terms of the time and effort required and can range from a certificate gained over a few days to a university course over several years which results in a degree.

People aged 15 and over attending university and other tertiary institutions, 2016

This map shows that people are more likely to attend university in the more urban and coastal parts of the country. This is because this is where most universities are located and, as we have seen in Chapter 24, where most Indigenous people live.

The number of Indigenous students enrolled in universities is fairly low but it is growing. This low number is partly due to the location of universities and partly to the limited secondary education facilities in remote areas.

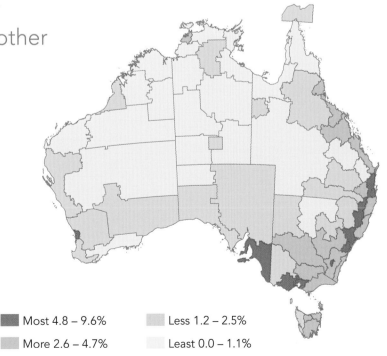

■ Most 4.8 – 9.6%   ■ Less 1.2 – 2.5%
■ More 2.6 – 4.7%   ■ Least 0.0 – 1.1%

Charles Perkins, Graduation Day
University of Sydney, NSW, 1966

Charles Perkins became one of Australia's first Indigenous university graduates in May 1966. During his time at university, he was one of the leaders of the civil rights movement known as the Freedom Rides. In later years, he went on to become the head of the Commonwealth Department of Aboriginal Affairs and was the first Indigenous Australian to hold such a senior position in the public service. For information on the Freedom Rides see Chapter 22.

WORD ALERT

civil rights

Civil rights are the rights of every citizen to personal freedom and equality.

The internet

The internet is now a well-established and vital technology. In the past, the different rates of use by Indigenous people likely reflected its availability. While access has expanded dramatically in recent years, it is still not Australia-wide. Where available in remote communities, it has become an important addition to daily life. Smartphones and other technologies have opened up access to communication, banking and other services that in the past were limited, or difficult to access. Access to the internet also opens up new learning opportunities, although as shown in the following map, this access is not the same over all of the country.

Percentage of dwellings with Indigenous residents having internet access, 2016

In capital cities, between about 75 and 88 per cent of residents have internet access. However, in remote desert areas in the centre, south and west of the continent, as few as 9 per cent of households have access to this increasingly vital technology.

■ Most 69.9 – 88.1%　　■ Less 37.2 – 53.9%

■ More 54.0 – 69.8%　　■ Least 8.9 – 37.1%

CHAPTER 26 Working life

Paid employment is a major key to economic wellbeing for all people. In the map titles in this chapter 'adult' refers to those people who are between 18 and 64 years old. This group of people is called the 'working-aged' population.

Patterns of employment

The economy is often looked at as being made up of three main areas or sectors. Different industries and jobs fall within each of these sectors.

- primary sector – industries which are involved in the growing, producing or extraction of natural resources
- secondary sector – industries which are involved in the production of manufactured goods
- tertiary sector – the part of the economy involved in providing services

We will also look at another sector which some people work in. It is often called the 'customary sector' and forms an important part of Indigenous lives and economy.

All of the maps in this chapter use the comparisons of Most ■, More ■, Less ■ and Least ■. A percentage range is given for each category.

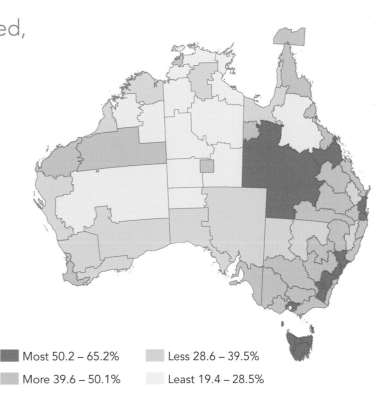

Adults who were employed, 2016

Overall, Indigenous employment is highest in Australia's largest cities and surrounding areas – where we find most industry. The high levels in Queensland are likely connected to employment in the mining industry. The high levels in Tasmania likely reflect the recent growth in tourism there.

Employment is generally lowest in remote regions, although levels are quite high in Torres Strait, Cape York, and the Pilbara. The Pilbara levels may also be due to employment in the mining industry.

Most 50.2 – 65.2%
More 39.6 – 50.1%
Less 28.6 – 39.5%
Least 19.4 – 28.5%

Percentage of the employed working in primary industries, 2016

The primary sector includes industries such as farming, forestry and mining. These are mainly found in rural areas away from cities. Farming of sheep, cattle and other animals for their meat or wool employs many people in large parts of Western Australia, South Australia and western Queensland. Although mining and animal farming are important industries in the Northern Territory, fewer people seem to be employed in them there.

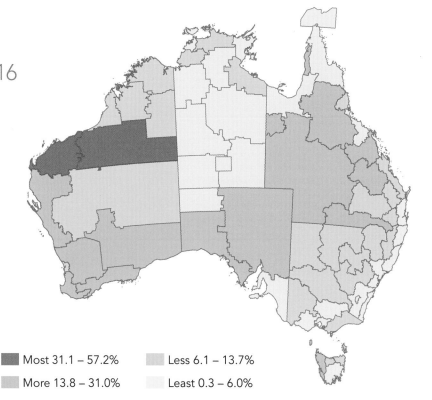

Most 31.1 – 57.2%

More 13.8 – 31.0%

Less 6.1 – 13.7%

Least 0.3 – 6.0%

Breaking in a horse

Gunbalanya, Arnhem Land, NT, 1950

Horses which hadn't been ridden before needed to be trained to carry a rider and wear a saddle and bridle. This process is called 'breaking in'.

This photo shows a stockman working on a station in the process of 'breaking in' a horse.

🔊 HOW DO YOU SAY IT?

Gunbalanya
gun–buh–**lun**–yuh

Percentage of the employed working in secondary industries, 2016

The secondary sector includes industries such as manufacturing, construction and the supply of electricity, gas and water. The pattern of employment in this map shows that this industry sector is mostly in the urban and eastern parts of the country – the most industrialised parts of Australia.

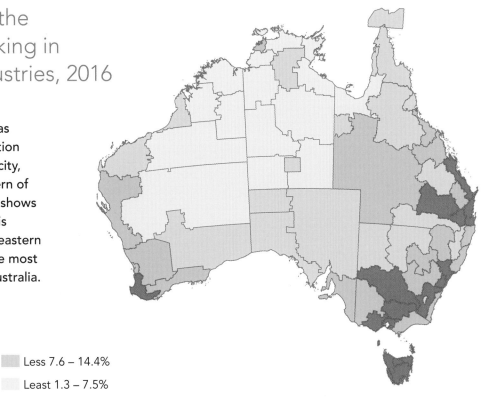

■ Most 21.3 – 25.8%		☐ Less 7.6 – 14.4%
■ More 14.5 – 21.2%		☐ Least 1.3 – 7.5%

Percentage of the employed working in tertiary industries, 2016

The tertiary – or third – part of the economy provides services. It includes industries such as transport, communications, education, health, banking, waste disposal and information technology (IT).

Indigenous employment in this sector is highest over most of the Northern Territory, in the Fitzroy River Valley, the Gulf Country, Cape York Peninsula and Torres Strait. If you compare this map to the previous two maps you will see that employment in tertiary industries is highest in areas where people's employment in the primary or secondary industries is lowest.

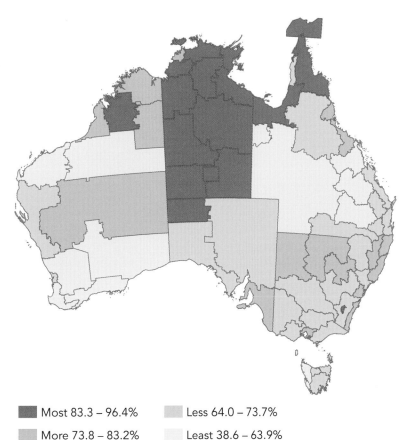

■ Most 83.3 – 96.4%		☐ Less 64.0 – 73.7%
■ More 73.8 – 83.2%		☐ Least 38.6 – 63.9%

Indigenous businesses

The number of Indigenous businesses has risen in recent years, even more than other Australian businesses. This rise is partly due to a 2015 government policy which encouraged the government departments to buy goods and services from Indigenous businesses. The rise may also be due to support from the Indigenous Chambers of Commerce which are organisations that support business people across Australia.

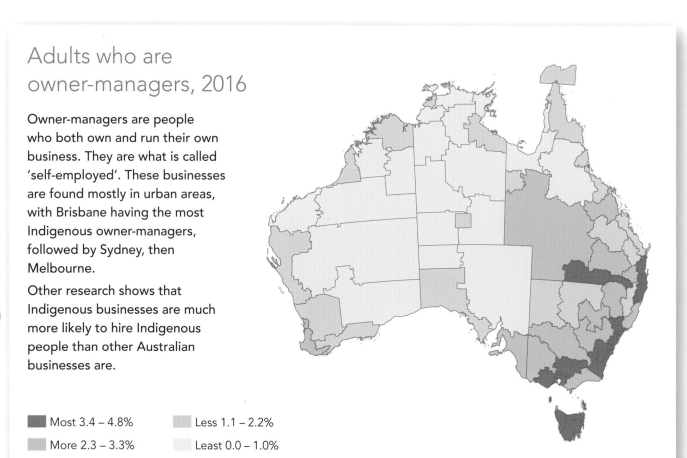

Adults who are owner-managers, 2016

Owner-managers are people who both own and run their own business. They are what is called 'self-employed'. These businesses are found mostly in urban areas, with Brisbane having the most Indigenous owner-managers, followed by Sydney, then Melbourne.

Other research shows that Indigenous businesses are much more likely to hire Indigenous people than other Australian businesses are.

- ■ Most 3.4 – 4.8%
- ■ More 2.3 – 3.3%
- ■ Less 1.1 – 2.2%
- ■ Least 0.0 – 1.0%

The customary sector

Activities carried out in what is often called the 'customary sector' focus on more than just profit and production. They form a significant part of many Indigenous people's lives and are intertwined with cultural traditions and cultural obligations.

Some of these activities include:

- hunting and gathering of wildlife, fish, bush foods and plants
- caring for Country
- conservation of resources
- traditional fire management of land
- collection of materials to produce art and artefacts for sale

Adults engaged in hunting, fishing and gathering, 2014–2015

People hunt, fish and gather bush foods much as they did in pre-contact times, although modern techniques are sometimes now used. To hunt, fish and to gather bush foods people need access to the land and waters – to their Country. If you compare this map with the maps in Chapter 18, you can see that this activity is very high where people also have ownership or some control over access to the land and waters.

This map shows that activity is also quite high in some coastal areas – where access is easier for all citizens. Hunting, fishing and gathering is much less common in urban areas, but even there, the rates are still quite high with 34 to 43 percent of people taking part.

Generally, people are not paid for this work. They eat what they get and also share it with their families. And so, although hunting, fishing and gathering is a form of income, it is also a very important social and cultural activity for Indigenous people and one that is closely associated with control of and access to land. This is also true for the 'caring for Country' strategies that are in Chapter 19 and the commercial sale of art in Chapter 13.

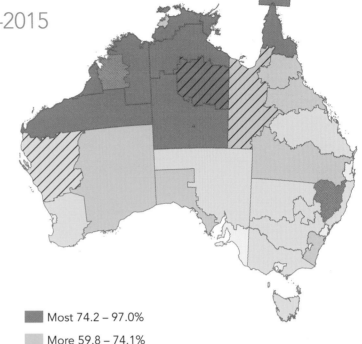

■ Most 74.2 – 97.0%
■ More 59.8 – 74.1%
■ Less 43.5 – 59.7%
■ Least 34.1 – 43.4%
/// Interpret with care
▨ Insufficient data

FAST FACT

Mutton birds are also harvested for their feathers and natural oils.

Muttonbirders Jason Thomas, Terry Maynard and David Maluga
Photographer: Ricky Maynard, Babel Island, Tasmania, 1970s

The mutton bird is a type of seabird of the southern oceans. Mutton bird eggs and meat were regular sources of food for Indigenous Tasmanians in pre-contact times. Muttonbirding became an industry in the 1820s when seal hunting was in decline. They are now harvested commercially in Tasmania.

Harvesting cycad
Central Arnhem Land, NT, 2003

This photo shows a ranger digging up a cycad for commercial sale. It is part of the Djelk Community Ranger Program which is based at Maningrida in central Arnhem Land. The rangers are working with Charles Darwin University to develop projects for the sustainable harvesting of indigenous plants and wildlife. More information on rangers and the distribution of their programs can be found in Chapter 19.

Hunters North-central Arnhem Land, NT, 1980

The men in this photo are using both introduced and traditional hunting weapons. The man on the left is carrying a spearthrower and two spears. The other men are carrying rifles. While people still carry out customary activities, new technologies are sometimes utilised.

Toyota with fish trap
North-central Arnhem Land, NT, 1980

This photo shows a four-wheel drive carrying a group of people – young and old – and an intricate fish trap. It is likely the people were all related. Four-wheel drives are used extensively in Arnhem Land to travel between settlements and for hunting, fishing and gathering trips. They allow people to travel with their equipment to areas rich in resources which are a long distance away. The photo was taken in 1980 when people often travelled in the open backs of vehicles, when they had access to them.

CHAPTER 27

Health and wellbeing

In pre-contact times, people relied on their detailed knowledge of the medicinal properties of native flora and fauna to treat health problems. There were, and still are, men and women who are acknowledged as expert healers in the physical, spiritual and emotional realms. Today, several health services employ traditional healers to work alongside their medical staff. To keep healthy, people need to have access to quality health care, and then to actively seek out and use the available services.

The health of Indigenous Australians was severely affected by the process of colonisation. Introduced diseases and drug substances had a dramatic impact. Poor and incomplete data has made it difficult to map nationwide patterns and trends in Indigenous health and mortality.

Introduced diseases

The people on the First Fleet from England and those who came afterward brought many new diseases to Australia, such as influenza, tuberculosis, measles and leprosy. Smallpox is also thought to have been brought to Australia by the Macassans.

Introduced diseases in the 1700s and 1800s

All of the introduced diseases shown in this map had a fatal impact on Indigenous people. Most known cases were in the south and east of the country, possibly reflecting the spread of colonisation from Sydney.

The first case of smallpox ■ in the Sydney region was in 1789, a year after the First Fleet arrived. It may have caused the death of up to 30 per cent of the Indigenous population that had contact with the newcomers. The first outbreak of influenza ●, also at Sydney, was in 1836. It quickly spread to the west and south to Melbourne, Tasmania and South Australia. Measles ▲ mostly affected people in Victoria and parts of South Australia, where some settlements lost up to 20 per cent of the population. Malaria ◆ was introduced to the Darwin region sometime in the 1800s.

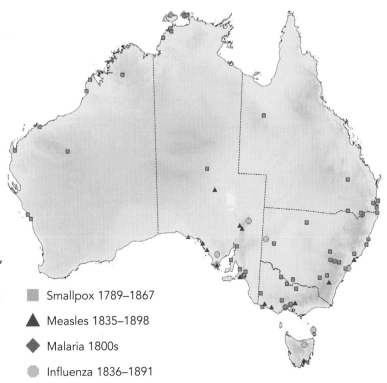

■ Smallpox 1789–1867

▲ Measles 1835–1898

◆ Malaria 1800s

● Influenza 1836–1891

Introduced diseases in the 1900s

The Spanish influenza ● pandemic (or Spanish flu) of 1918 killed at least 315 people in Queensland, and unknown numbers of others in the rest of the country. Between 1947 and 1951 measles ▲ swept through the Northern Territory and South Australia, again causing heavy mortality. Leprosy arrived and affected people across the north from the 1880s. Sufferers were isolated in treatment centres for leprosy which were called leprosaria ■. These were often on offshore islands such as Channel Island near Darwin, Fantome Island in Queensland, and Bernier and Dorre Islands in Shark Bay, Western Australia. There was also a centre near Mowanjum in the Kimberley.

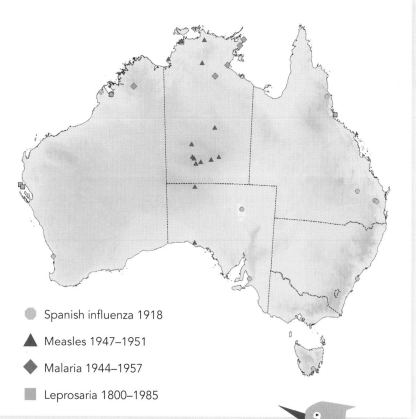

● Spanish influenza 1918

▲ Measles 1947–1951

◆ Malaria 1944–1957

■ Leprosaria 1800–1985

Dangerous substances

Indigenous Australians knew of and used mild alcoholic drinks, tobacco and other mood-altering drugs before the arrival of Europeans. Some drugs were introduced from outside and some were locally produced.

Species

▨ *Nicotiana benthamiana*

▨ *Nicotiana excelsior*

▧ *Nicotiana gossei*

▨ *Nicotiana rosulata*

FAST FACT

*Another name for a traditional healer is ngangkari. You say it **ngung**-guh-ree. It comes from Pitjantjatjara, a language of SA.*

Four types of bush tobacco

Sixteen known native tobaccos grow on the Australian mainland. This map shows the distribution of the four most used species which are found mainly in the arid and semi-arid zones. The leaves of certain species are dried, ground and mixed with ash. They are then chewed in small portions called 'quids'. People used tube-like pipes to smoke bush tobacco in parts of Queensland and South Australia close to the Georgina River, the Diamantina River and Cooper Creek.

'Pitjuri' and intoxicating drinks

In an area running north to south down the borders of Queensland and South Australia, people used a natural drug substance called *pitjuri*. This is prepared from the dried leaves of a native shrub which, like the tobacco mentioned earlier, are mixed with ash and chewed. *Pitjuri* was also traded along the routes shown in the map. Trading centres were established in the region around the present-day Bedourie and Birdsville, and would sometimes attract up to 500 people.

People also made mildly intoxicating drinks from at least nine different species of flora which occur in the areas shown. The palm syrup drink 'tuba' and its name was introduced to Torres Strait by people from the Philippines.

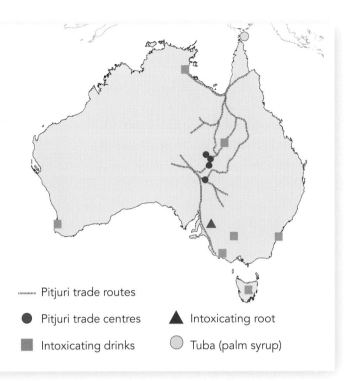

····· Pitjuri trade routes

● Pitjuri trade centres   ▲ Intoxicating root

■ Intoxicating drinks   ● Tuba (palm syrup)

Introduced types of pipes

The Macassans brought tobacco and opium pipes 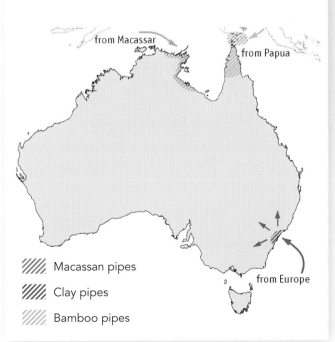 to northern Australia from around 1720. Tobacco and clay pipes arrived in south-eastern Australia with the First Fleet in 1788. These British clay pipes became popular with Aboriginal people all across the country in the 1800s. Bamboo pipes came into Torres Strait and northern Queensland from present-day Papua New Guinea.

from Macassar

from Papua

from Europe

▨ Macassan pipes

▨ Clay pipes

▨ Bamboo pipes

Bamboo pipes Torres Strait, around 1900

These illustrations show tobacco pipes from Torres Strait. They were similar to those from neighbouring Papua New Guinea. These pipes could be between 50 and 90 cm long. Tobacco called *lamlam* grew wild on Mer Island.

Smoking a Macassan pipe
Central Arnhem Land, NT, 1978

The Macassan style of pipe shown in this photo is still used today, especially by older people.

Today, drinking alcohol has become a problem for some people. Although many Indigenous Australians do not drink alcohol at all, those who do are more likely to do so at dangerous levels. Risky drinking is more common among people living in non-remote areas, because people in remote areas have the option of declaring their communities as 'dry', which means alcohol-free. It is not possible to do this in cities or rural towns. Alcohol abuse is associated with poor health and reduced lifespan and often plays a part in road accidents and assaults. It is also associated with family breakdown and violence as well as financial and legal problems.

FAST FACT

There are more than 100 dry communities in the Northern Territory. South Australia, Western Australia and Queensland also have dry communities.

Some terms for alcohol

People referred to the introduced alcohol in words from their own language. These were often words which described how the drink tasted to them. In the dryer and central regions, words meaning *sweet* or *delicious* ■ were used. In some northern coastal regions and around Lake Eyre in South Australia, words meaning *salty*, *bitter* or *sour* ■ were used. Describing alcohol with words meaning *dangerous*, *bad* or *poisonous* ■ was found in several scattered locations.

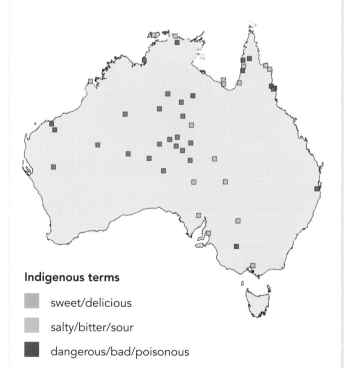

Indigenous terms

■ sweet/delicious

■ salty/bitter/sour

■ dangerous/bad/poisonous

The pregnancy poster
Artist: Marie McMahon, 1988

This health education poster illustrates the message that unborn children are affected by the drinking and smoking of pregnant women. It is done in the style of 'x-ray' art which is looked at in Chapter 13.

FAST FACT

*The NPY in NPY Women's Council stands for **Ngaanyatjarra Pitjantjatjara Yankunytjatjara**.*

Women from the NPY Women's Council protest alcohol sales
Coober Pedy, SA, 2008

Indigenous women in many regions have spoken out about the effects of alcohol abuse on their families, and have taken to the streets to demonstrate against violence and to demand restrictions on alcohol sales. This photo shows women demonstrating in Coober Pedy, where takeaway liquor sales affect the wellbeing of the local communities.

Since the 1970s, the deliberate inhalation of petrol fumes has been a damaging form of drug use among younger people. Petrol sniffing has caused hospitalisations, brain damage and some deaths. The practice spread to an increasing number of communities. In 2005, a low-aromatic lead-free fuel called Opal was made available. It lacked the ingredients which produced the 'high' sought by sniffers. A large number of remote communities and nearby petrol stations replaced their standard fuel with Opal and the number of people sniffing petrol dropped dramatically.

You can help stop petrol sniffing
Artist: Liam Campbell, 2005

This postcard was part of a campaign asking the federal government for more funding to make low-aromatic fuel available in all regions and major towns affected by petrol sniffing.

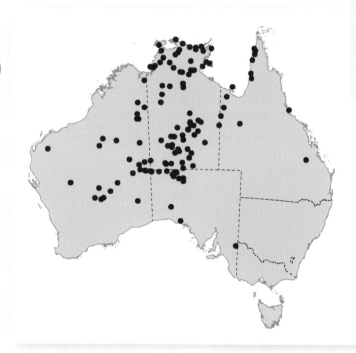

Where low-aromatic fuel is available, 2018

Low-aromatic fuel is now widely available in regional and remote areas. By 2018 it was sold at 175 sites across the mainly remote areas of Queensland, the Northern Territory, Western Australia and South Australia.

● Sites where low-aromatic fuel is available

Dialysis

The leading cause of hospitalisation for Indigenous people is the need for dialysis for the treatment of a serious condition called chronic renal disease. This disease means that a person's kidneys are badly damaged and don't function properly. Dialysis is used to filter out damaging waste products from the blood. A person experiencing chronic renal disease needs either dialysis or a kidney transplant to keep living.

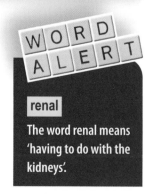

WORD ALERT

renal
The word renal means 'having to do with the kidneys'.

Indigenous patients on dialysis for kidney disease, 2016

This map shows that the greatest number of people on dialysis for kidney disease are in the remote parts of the country. However, the equipment needed to do kidney transplants is only available in hospitals in the cities in the south or south-east of the country.

Estimated number of patients

0.0 – 1.0	5.1 – 10.0	50.1 – 100.0
1.1 – 2.0	10.1 – 20.0	100.1 – 200.0
2.1 – 5.0	20.1 – 50.0	200.1 – 300.0

The Purple Truck mobile dialysis unit Alice Springs, NT, 2012

The Purple Truck is a fully-functioning dialysis unit on wheels. It has two dialysis chairs and travels to around 20 remote communities in a year. It also helps patients who are on dialysis in Alice Springs to return home for visits to family. This has helped to reduce the isolation that many dialysis patients feel when they have to move away from their homelands, their language and their culture for treatment. The Purple Truck is funded by art auctions, donations and with the support of private foundations.

Trachoma

Trachoma is a painful eye disease that causes blindness if left untreated. It has been found in Australia since at least the late 1700s and originally affected both Indigenous and non-Indigenous people – the early colonists called it the 'Sandy Blight' because it felt like the eyes were full of sand. In the 1940s and 1950s, it was found that up to 90 per cent of Aboriginal people in Central Australia had the disease.

Antibiotics and a focus on facial cleanliness and environmental improvements has resulted in a drop in the cases of trachoma – from 21 per cent in 2008 to just 4.6 per cent in 2015. Eye doctors now say we are close to eliminating the disease.

◀) HOW DO YOU SAY IT?

trachoma
truh–koh–muh

Trachoma, 2015

Trachoma is found mostly in the remote and very remote communities of the Northern Territory, South Australia and Western Australia, although there are small pockets of the disease in New South Wales and Queensland. Australia is the only developed country in which trachoma still occurs.

☐ Not at risk

☐ No trachoma detected

☐ 5% to less than 10%

☐ Less than 5%

■ 10% to less than 20%

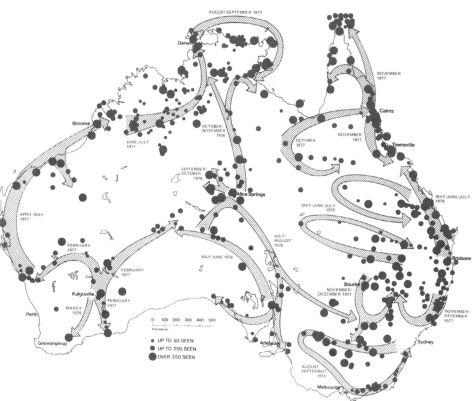

Movement of the National Trachoma and Eye Health Program teams, 1977–1979

In 1976, the National Trachoma and Eye Health Program began, led by the late Professor Fred Hollows. Its teams travelled thousands of kilometres by road across Australia to screen and treat the disease. This work continues today.

Wellbeing

Aboriginal and Torres Strait Islander people established their own primary health care services in the 1970s. They were called Aboriginal community-controlled health services, or ACCHS for short. They were created in response to the poor health status experienced by Indigenous people and the barriers they faced in accessing quality health care. Today, there are 141 ACCHS, and they are an essential part of the Australian health system. An ACCHS is usually run by Indigenous representatives from the local area. This means that communities can have control over planning, resources and services.

There are also social and emotional wellbeing services available, or SEWB for short. They are often attached to, or part of an ACCHS. These are services designed to help people to deal with grief and loss, trauma and life-threatening thoughts, as well as the stresses of daily life.

Indigenous-focused aged-care programs, 2016–2017

Indigenous-focused aged-care programs are found very much in the remote centre and north of the country. Others are distributed along the east and south-east coasts. Most people make use of home support and home-care programs, but in remote or very remote areas there are live-in homes where more than half of the residents are Indigenous. These remote aged-care homes provide cultural safety and security for their residents. They are often in or near communities so that family members can visit. This is important, as half of their residents have dementia.

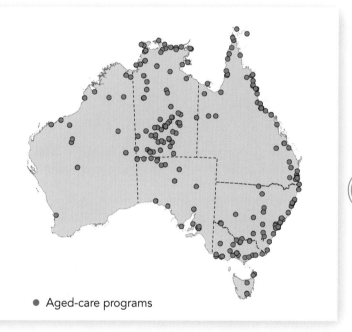

● Aged-care programs

Aboriginal community-controlled primary health care services, 2016

Aboriginal community-controlled health services (ACCHS) ● were originally set up where the Indigenous population was greatest, but with population growth they have spread to more parts of the country. Although these services are generally well-positioned across the country, there are still areas where there is no Indigenous-specific service within one hour's drive of home, and where access to a doctor is limited.

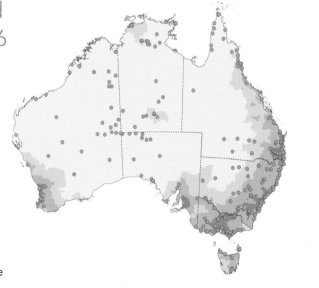

● ACCHS	▮ Inner regional	▮ Remote
▮ Major cities	▮ Outer regional	▮ Very remote

Organisations providing social and emotional wellbeing support, 2016–2017

Although there are some social and emotional wellbeing services (SEWB) ● in the remoter parts of the country, in 2016 almost half were located in New South Wales, the Australian Capital Territory and Queensland. A service called Link-Up ● assists people who were separated from their families by former laws to trace and reunite with their relatives. These Link-Up services are in all states and territories except Tasmania and the Australian Capital Territory.

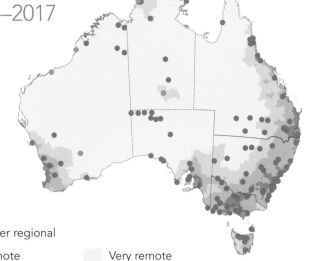

● SEWB support services
● Link-Up services

	Major cities
	Inner regional
	Outer regional
	Remote
	Very remote

Uti Kulintjaku Artist: Joshua Santospiritu Design: Elliat Rich, 2017

Indigenous organisations are creating new ways to support emotional and mental health needs. One way to improve understanding of mental health is by finding the best words to describe feelings, memories and emotions. This poster is part of an exercise to communicate such words, developed by a group of senior women of the APY Women's Council. The group is called Uti Kulintjaku which means 'to think and understand clearly'. They are concerned about family wellbeing. Its members come together to explore health ideas from both Western and Indigenous perspectives and so enable people to ask for the help they need.

🔊 HOW DO YOU SAY IT?

Uti Kulintjaku
yooh–tee
koo–lin–jah–gooh

Location of Indigenous doctors, midwives and nurses, 2016

This map shows that the vast majority of Indigenous health professionals are found in the coastal centres of the east and south-east where there are high populations, and very few in the more remote parts.

Persons

- Most 187–407
- More 97–186
- Less 39–96
- Least 0–38

In 2004 there were 90 Indigenous doctors, and by 2014 this number had increased to 204. However, to reach the same proportion of doctors to people as in the general population, the number needs to be greatly increased. The Australian Indigenous Doctors Association continues to push for more Indigenous health professionals. In 2015 there were more than 3000 Indigenous nurses or midwives.

WORD ALERT

telehealth

Telehealth is the name for health services which people access by telephone or by video call over the internet.

155

Flight paths of the Royal Flying Doctor Service, 2016

This map shows where the Royal Flying Doctor Service operates from and its travel routes. The Royal Flying Doctor Service was founded in 1928 and provides emergency and primary health care to people in remote areas. It is a charitable not-for-profit organisation and its services are free. It operates a round-the-clock telehealth service, runs regular health clinics and airlifts emergency cases to hospitals. Many Indigenous people receive their health care through this invaluable service.

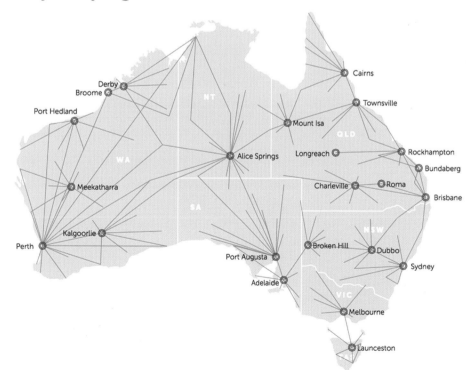

Appendixes

156

A note for teachers on mapping conventions and geographies

For examples of the map types see Chapter 1.

Thematic maps have been carried over unchanged – or with minor updates – from the second edition of the *Macquarie Atlas of Indigenous Australia*. Choropleth maps and some thematic maps were produced by the Centre of Aboriginal and Torres Strait Islander Statistics and the Geospatial Solutions sections of the Australian Bureau of Statistics (ABS), Canberra, who also provided information for this Note.

Maps were created using the Geocentric Datum of Australia 1994 (GDA94) Albers Equal Area Conic projection, with a central meridian of 135° east and standard parallels of 18° and 36° south, was specified. The map unit is meters and there is no false origin shift. All maps are orientated conventionally with north at the top of the image. National maps are presented at a scale of 1:46,796,556. Detailed maps, such as those for zoomed-in areas, are shown at a variety of scales.

Choropleth maps were produced using the system of Natural Breaks (Jenks). In this system the data-classes are based on the natural groupings inherent in the data; where classes with similar values are collected together and the differences between classes are maximised. The quality of the representation of this type of map depends to some extent on the quality of the data and on the number and size of the areas on the map.

Choropleth geographies

The choropleth maps were produced to customised geographies derived from the standard ABS Indigenous Structure and its associated geographies (see http://www.abs.gov.au/ausstats/abs@.nsf/mf/1270.0.55.002), and are described below.

Choropleth maps derived from the 2016 Census

The most recent national Census of Population and Housing for which data are available for this Atlas was held in 2016. For this the ABS developed strategies to ensure that the coverage of Indigenous people across Australia was as complete as possible. For the Atlas a special geography was constructed, in collaboration with the ABS, for mapping census data. It consolidated many of the 430 Indigenous Areas (IAREs) of the 2016 Census geography into some 69 regions. It also included customised shapes for the area around Alice Springs and for Torres Strait. The boundaries of this type of map are shown in Map A1. Most of these are dated 2016. However, in a number of cases the maps show the change that has occurred between several censuses, and these carry the relevant dates. Census-based maps are in Chapters 1, 16, 24, 25, 26, and 27.

157

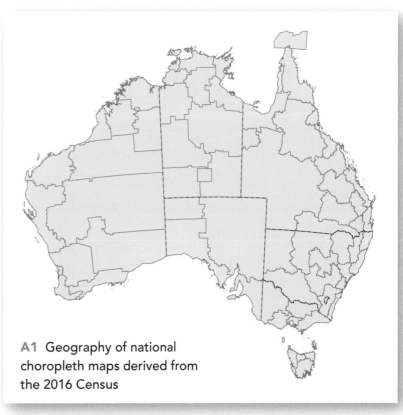

A1 Geography of national choropleth maps derived from the 2016 Census

Choropleth maps derived from the NATSISS 2014–2015

The National Aboriginal and Torres Strait Islander Social Survey (NATSISS) was carried out by the ABS over 2014–2015. The NATSISS surveyed a sample of 11 178 Indigenous people, weighted to infer results for the whole population and designed to produce reliable estimates at the national level, for each state and territory, and by remoteness area. The ABS produced two geographies to map the NATSISS data for this Atlas. One was based on the ABS standard 2011 geography of 57 Indigenous Regions (IREGs) but included a customised shape to show Torres Strait. The second geography also included the Torres Strait shape but in addition consolidated several of the more rural regions. Several of the areas in these maps contain data with a relative standard error (RSE) of 25–50 per cent; these areas are shown hatched, and are labelled 'Interpret with care' in the key. For other areas that have data with an RSE of greater than 50 per

cent, the data are not mapped; the areas are shaded grey on the map, and are labelled in the map key as 'Insufficient data'. NATSISS-based maps drawn to these two geographies are dated 2014–2015 and are in Chapters 1, 11, 21, and 26.

The regional names used in the Atlas to describe all national choropleth maps are shown in Map A2.

Maps derived from the CHINS 2006

In 2006 the ABS carried out the Community Housing and Infrastructure Needs Survey (CHINS). This was a survey of all discrete Indigenous communities and organisations that provide housing to Indigenous people. It covered a total of 496 organisations and 1187 discrete communities nationally. Maps that use these data carry the date 2006 and are in Chapters 1 and 24.

Other map geographies

- Details of the remoteness areas shown in Chapters 20, 24 and 27 are at http://www.abs.gov.au/websitedbs/D3310114.nsf/home/remoteness+structure

- The boundaries of the trachoma prevalence map in Chapter 27 were supplied by the Kirby Institute at the University of New South Wales.

- Maps in Chapter 18 that show areas of land associated with Native Title matters are sourced from the National Native Title Tribunal, and are constructed by the Tribunal using geographies relevant to the particular topic.

A2 Regional names used to describe national choropleth maps

Pronunciation Guide

This table is a key to the pronunciation guides which are given in the HOW DO YOU SAY IT? sections in the Atlas.

In this table, the sounds have been divided into vowels and consonants. The vowels have been grouped roughly according to sound, for ease of use.

Consonants which are pronounced in the usual way (p, b, s, z, etc.) are not included in this key.

Vowels	**a** sounds	**e** sounds
	a as in 'pat'	*e* as in 'pet'
	ah as in 'part'	*ee* as in 'feet'
	ay as in 'bay'	*air* as in 'pair'
	i sounds	**o** sounds
	i as in 'pit'	*o* as in 'pot'
	uy as in 'buy'	*oh* as in 'boat'
	ear as in 'hear'	*aw* as in 'paw'
		ow as in 'how'
	u sounds	*oy* as in 'boy'
	u as in 'but'	
	oo as in 'book'	**er** sounds
	ooh as in 'boot'	*er* as in 'pert'
	oouh as in 'tour'	*uh* as in 'matt**er**'

Consonants	*th* as in 'thin'	*ch* as in 'chase'
	dh as in 'then'	*j* as in 'jug'
	sh as in 'show'	*g* as in 'game'
	zh as in 'measure'	*ng* as in 'sing'

Stress	Bold (thick) letters show the part of the word that is said with more stress than the other parts of the word.
	For example, **at**–luhs as in 'atlas'

Abbreviations used in the Atlas

ABS	Australian Bureau of Statistics
ACCHS	Aboriginal community-controlled health service(s)
ACT	Australian Capital Territory
AFL	Australian Football League
AIATSIS	Australian Institute of Aboriginal and Torres Strait Islander Studies
ALRA	*Aboriginal Land Rights (Northern Territory) Act 1976*
APY	Anangu Pitjantjatjara Yankunytjatjara
BRACS	Broadcasting for Remote Aboriginal Communities Scheme
cm	centimetre(s)
E	east
GPS	Global Positioning System
ILUA	Indigenous Land Use Agreement
IPA	Indigenous Protected Area
IT	information technology
km²	square kilometre(s)
N	north
NATSISS	National Aboriginal and Torres Strait Islander Social Survey
NE	north-east
NITV	National Indigenous Television
NPY	Ngaanyatjarra Pitjantjatjara Yankunytjatjara
NRL	National Rugby League
NSW	New South Wales
NT	Northern Territory
NW	north-west
PNG	Papua New Guinea
Qld	Queensland
S	south
SA	South Australia
SE	south-east
SEWB	social and emotional wellbeing
SW	south-west
USA	United States of America
W	west
WA	Western Australia

Authors

The *Junior Atlas of Indigenous Australia* is based upon the two editions of the *Macquarie Atlas of Indigenous Australia*. The content has been adapted to suit a younger audience by the General Editors, Bill Arthur from the Centre for Aboriginal Economic Policy Research (CAEPR) at the Australian National University and Victoria Morgan, Managing Editor from Macquarie Dictionary Publishers. It includes contributions from more than 40 authors from a wide variety of places and professions – from universities, the arts world, Indigenous organisations and the public service. The following are the authors who contributed to one or other of the editions, and their affiliations at the time of their contribution.

Jon Altman Centre for Aboriginal Economic Policy Research (CAEPR), Australian National University.

Bill Arthur Centre for Aboriginal Economic Policy Research (CAEPR), Australian National University.

Linda Barwick Music Department, University of Sydney, and PARADISEC (Pacific and Regional Archive for Digital Sources in Endangered Cultures).

Maggie Brady Centre for Aboriginal Economic Policy Research (CAEPR), Australian National University.

Heather Crawford Centre for Aboriginal Economic Policy Research (CAEPR), Australian National University.

Tony Dreise Tony is a proud descendant of the Guumilroi (Gamilaraay) and Euahlayi (Yuwaalaraay) First Nations peoples of north-west New South Wales and south-west Queensland. Centre for Aboriginal Economic Policy Research (CAEPR), Australian National University.

Dennis Foley Dennis is of Gai-mariagal and Wiradjuri descent. Faculty of Business, Government and Law, University of Canberra.

Donna Green Climate Change Research Centre, ARC Centre of Excellence for Climate Extremes, and the NHMRC Centre for Energy, Air Pollution and Health Research, University of New South Wales.

Boyd Hunter Centre for Social Research and Methods, Australian National University, and Australian Society of Labour Economics.

Glenn Iseger-Pilkington Glenn is a Nhanda, Wadjarri and Noongar man from the mid-west and south-west of Western Australia. GEE CONSULTANCY.

Diana James Research School of Humanities and the Arts, Australian National University.

Dianne Johnson Author.

Roger Jones Consultant.

Barry Judd Barry is a descendant of the Pitjantjatjara people of north-west South Australia, British immigrants and Afghan cameleers. Office of Pro Vice-Chancellor Indigenous Leadership, Charles Darwin University, and University of Western Australia.

Grace Koch Australian Institute of Aboriginal and Torres Strait Islander Studies (AIATSIS).

Harold Koch School of Literature, Language and Linguistics, Australian National University.

Kim Mahood Author, artist, and consultant.

Francis Markham Centre for Aboriginal Economic Policy Research (CAEPR), Australian National University.

Virginia Marshall Virginia is Wiradjuri Nyemba and the first Indigenous Postdoctoral Fellow with the Schools of Regulation and Global Governance, and Fenner School of Environment and Society, Australian National University.

Patrick McConvell Australian Institute of Aboriginal and Torres Strait Islander Studies (AIATSIS).

Frances Morphy Centre for Aboriginal Economic Policy Research (CAEPR), Australian National University.

Howard Morphy Research School of Humanities and the Arts, College of Arts and Social Sciences, Australian National University.

Kingsley Palmer Consultant anthropologist.

Yin Paradies Yin is an Aboriginal-Anglo-Asian Australian from the Northern Territory. Menzies School of Health Research.

Huw Peacock Huw is a palawa man, descended from the pairrebenne people of north-east lutruwita (Tasmania). Aboriginal Research and Leadership, University of Tasmania.

Nicolas Peterson School of Archaeology and Anthropology, Australian National University.

Kellie Pollard Kellie is of the Wiradjuri and Githabul (Gidhabal) Indigenous Nations of rural New South Wales. College of Indigenous Futures, Arts and Society, Charles Darwin University.

Peter Radoll Peter is a descendant of the Anaiwan People of northern New South Wales. Office of Aboriginal and Torres Strait Islander Leadership and Strategy, and the Ngunnawal Centre at the University of Canberra. Centre of Economic Policy Research, Australian National University.

Tim Rowse Institute for Culture and Society, Western Sydney University, and the National Centre for Biography, Australian National University.

Lyndall Ryan School of Humanities and Social Sciences, University of Newcastle.

Chris Sainsbury Chris is a member of the Dharug nation. School of Music, Australian National University.

Will Sanders Centre for Aboriginal Economic Policy Research (CAEPR), Australian National University.

Leonn Satterthwait Anthropology Museum, University of Queensland.

Jane Simpson Australian Research Council Centre of Excellence for the Dynamics of Language, Australian National University.

R. G. (Jerry) Schwab Centre for Aboriginal Economic Policy Research (CAEPR), Australian National University.

Claire Smith College of Humanities, Arts and Social Sciences, Flinders University.

Mike Smith College of Humanities, Arts and Social Sciences, Flinders University, and the National Museum of Australia.

Dale Sutherland Dale is a member of the Minjungbal people of the Bundjalung nation, from the Tweed Valley and coast of far northern New South Wales. Australian Indigenous Governance Institute.

John Taylor Centre for Aboriginal Economic Research (CAEPR), Australian National University.

Luke Taylor Australian Institute of Aboriginal and Torres Strait Islander Studies (AIATSIS), and Centre for Cross-Cultural Research, Australian National University.

Nicholas Thieberger Department of Linguistics and Applied Linguistics, University of Melbourne.

Alan Thorne Department of Archaeology and Natural History, College of Asia and the Pacific, Australian National University.

Maggie Walter Maggie is palawa, descending from the pairrebenne people of north-east lutruwita (Tasmania) and a member of the larger Briggs Johnson Tasmanian Aboriginal family. Aboriginal Research and Leadership, University of Tasmania.

Daryl Wesley College of Humanities, Arts and Social Sciences, Flinders University.

Eunice Yu Eunice is a Yawuru and Bunuba woman. Yawuru Jarndu Aboriginal Corporation, Broome.

General Editors of the Junior Atlas of Indigenous Australia

Honorary Associate Professor BILL ARTHUR began researching Indigenous affairs in the early 1980s. Much of his initial work was land-related and was carried out for Indigenous organisations such as the Kimberley Land Council and Marra Worra Worra Aboriginal Corporation in Fitzroy Crossing. Since 1990, his research has focused more on issues of economic development, autonomy and policy for Torres Strait Islanders in the Centre for Aboriginal Economic Policy Research (CAEPR) at the Australian National University, and with the Australian Institute for Aboriginal and Torres Strait Islander Studies. At CAEPR, Bill initiated the publication of the *Macquarie Atlas of Indigenous Australia*, of which he and Frances Morphy were General Editors, for both the first and second editions. For the *Junior Atlas of Indigenous Australia*, Bill collaborated with Victoria Morgan to select and adapt material to create an edition suitable for an audience in their upper primary and lower secondary school years.

VICTORIA MORGAN is the Managing Editor at Macquarie Dictionary. She has worked for Macquarie Dictionary since 2004 across the extensive Macquarie range. As language is continuously changing, it is a never-ending job trying to keep abreast of new terms, shifts in language and style of Australian English. She also manages the creation and content for state and national spelling bees and has authored content for language resource titles for the primary education years. Victoria was involved in both editions of the parent title, the *Macquarie Atlas of Indigenous Australia*, in the roles of Permissions Coordinator and Senior Editor. For the *Junior Atlas of Indigenous Australia*, Victoria collaborated with Bill Arthur to select and adapt material to create an edition suitable for an audience in their upper primary and lower secondary school years.

163

Education and Cultural Consultant of the Junior Atlas of Indigenous Australia

JASMINE SEYMOUR is a Dharug woman and a descendant of Maria Lock, daughter of Yarramundi, the Boorooberongal Elder who met Governor Phillip on the banks of the Hawkesbury River in 1791. She is a primary school teacher, Dharug community language teacher and activist, artist and a published author of children's books which integrate Dharug language throughout: *Baby Business*, which tells the story of a ceremony that welcomes a baby to Country and *Cooee Mittigar (Come Here Friend)*, which is an invitation to walk on Dharug Country. Jasmine provided valued educational and cultural advice to the General Editors of the *Junior Atlas of Indigenous Australia*.

Acknowledgements

Items are listed in the order they appear on each page. For illustrations, the originator of the image is credited and any further necessary permissions are acknowledged. Every reasonable effort was made to obtain permission for the use of images in this Atlas.

A number of maps in this Atlas were prepared by the Archaeological Computing Laboratory (ACL) at the University of Sydney. These are acknowledged as ACL.

A number of maps in this Atlas were prepared by the Australian Bureau of Statistics (ABS). These are acknowledged as ABS. Some maps also include the relevant date and data source, followed by the geography used.

Maps that have been modified since appearing in the *Macquarie Atlas of Indigenous Australia (2nd edition 2019)* are indicated by the word 'modified'.

Page	**Chapter 1** Exploring the Atlas	
2	Image	123freevectors.com
2	Map	Macquarie Dictionary Publishers.
3	Image	Courtesy of May Abernethy.
3	Image	Macquarie Dictionary Publishers.
4	Map	ACL.
5	Map	ABS map from 2016 Census; customised from Australian Statistical Geography 2016, Indigenous Areas.
5	Map	ABS map from the 2015 National Aboriginal and Torres Strait Islander Social Survey; to the 2011 Australian Statistical Geography, Indigenous Regions.
6	Map	ABS 2006 Community Housing and Infrastructure Needs Survey.

Page	**Chapter 2** Deep history	
9	Table	Macquarie Dictionary Publishers.
10	Image	Courtesy of Robert Bednarik.
10	Map	ACL, modified.
11	Image	Macquarie Dictionary Publishers.
11	Map	ACL.
12	Image	Macquarie Dictionary Publishers.
12	Image	Macquarie Dictionary Publishers.
13	Map	ACL.
13	Image	Macquarie Dictionary Publishers.
14	Image	Macquarie Dictionary Publishers.
14	Image	Macquarie Dictionary Publishers.
14	Image	Macquarie Dictionary Publishers.
14	Image	Dragi Markovic, National Museum of Australia.

Page	Chapter 5	Hunting, fishing and fighting
28	Image	Reproduced by permission of Dr Philip Jones and South Australian Museum.
28	Map	ACL.
29	Image	Reproduced by permission of Dr Philip Jones and South Australian Museum.
29	Map	ACL.
29	Image	Macquarie Dictionary Publishers.
30	Map	ACL.
30	Image	Macquarie Dictionary Publishers.
30	Map	ACL.
31	Image	Reproduced by permission of Paul Wright.
32	Map	ACL.
32	Image	Macleay Museum Collection, University of Sydney. Reproduced by permission of David Liddle.
32	Image	Ludo Kuipers. Reproduced by permission of OzOutback Internet Services.
33	Image	Macquarie Dictionary Publishers.
33	Map	ACL.
34	Image	Artist George Aldridge, 1988. Reproduced by permission of South Australian Museum.
34	Image	Reproduced by permission of National Library of Australia.
35	Image	Photographer D. F. Thomson, The Donald Thomson Ethnohistory Collection. Reproduced courtesy of the Thomson family and Museums Victoria.
35	Map	ACL.
35	Image	Macquarie Dictionary Publishers.
36	Map	ACL, modified.
37	Image	Macquarie Dictionary Publishers.
37	Image	This image is copyright. Reproduced by permission of University of Cambridge Museum of Archaeology and Anthropology (P.1148.ACH1).
37	Map	Reproduced by permission of Josephine Flood. ACL, modified.

Page	Chapter 6	Watercraft
38	Map	ACL.
39	Image	Photographer Herbert Basedow. National Museum of Australia. Reproduced with permission of the Larynuwa Aboriginal Corporation.
39	Image	State Library of New South Wales.
39	Image	Macquarie Dictionary Publishers.
40	Map	ACL, modified.
40	Image	Bill Arthur.

Page	Chapter 7 Shelters and housing	
41	Image	Illustration by Paul Memmott and Tim O'Rourke, Aboriginal Environments Research Centre, University of Queensland.
42	Image	E. Myoburg, John Oxley Library Collection, State Library of Queensland, neg. no. 8975.
42	Image	This image is copyright. Reproduced by permission of University of Cambridge Museum of Archaeology and Anthropology (P.807.ACH1).
42	Image	Robert Raymond. Reproduced with permission of the photographer's family.

Page	Chapter 8 Fire	
43	Map	ACL.
44	Image	Photograph by Shane Bailey. NAILSMA and Learning on Country Maningrida ILM.

Page	Chapter 9 Clothing and shell adornments	
45	Map	ACL.
45	Image	Reproduced by permission of South Australian Museum.
46	Map	ACL.
46	Image	Robert Tonkinson.
47	Map	ACL.
47	Image	Macquarie Dictionary Publishers.
47	Image	Macleay Museum Collection, University of Sydney. Reproduced by permission of David Liddle.
48	Image	This image is copyright. Reproduced by permission of University of Cambridge Museum of Archaeology and Anthropology (P.794.ACH1).
48	Image	Australian Government Department of the Environment and Energy.

Page	Chapter 10 Containers	
49	Map	ACL.
50	Image	Macleay Museum Collection, University of Sydney. Reproduced by permission of David Liddle.
50	Image	Courtesy of May Abernethy.
50	Image	Photographer D. F. Thomson, The Donald Thomson Ethnohistory Collection. Reproduced courtesy of the Thomson family and Museums Victoria.
51	Map	ACL.
51	Image	Macleay Museum Collection, University of Sydney. Reproduced by permission of David Liddle.
51	Image	Macleay Museum Collection, University of Sydney. Reproduced by permission of David Liddle.

Page	Chapter 11 Cultural and religious life	
52	Map	ABS map from the 2015 National Aboriginal and Torres Strait Islander Social Survey; to the 2011 Australian Statistical Geography, Indigenous Regions. ABS, modified.
52	Map	ABS map from the 2015 National Aboriginal and Torres Strait Islander Social Survey; to the 2011 Australian Statistical Geography, Indigenous Regions.
52	Map	ABS map from the 2015 National Aboriginal and Torres Strait Islander Social Survey; to the 2011 Australian Statistical Geography, Indigenous Regions. ABS, modified.
53	Map	ACL, modified.
54	Map	ACL.
55	Image	Howard Morphy. Reproduced by permission of Wanyubi and Waninya Marika.
55	Image	Photographer Yngve Laurell, First Swedish Scientific Expedition to Australia 1910–1911. Courtesy of National Museum of Ethnography, Stockholm.
56	Map	ACL, modified.
56	Image	Bill Arthur.
57	Map	ACL.

Page	Chapter 12 Performing arts	
58	Map	ACL.
58	Image	Howard Morphy.
59	Map	ACL, modified.
59	Map	ACL.
60	Map	ACL.
60	Image	Courtesy of AIATSIS, Alice Moyle Collection, item MOYLE.A14.CS-166620. Reproduced by permission of Dr Alice Moyle's daughter, Dr Carolyn Lowry and 'Butcher' Joe Nangan's granddaughter, Brigid Drummond.
60	Image	Macquarie Dictionary Publishers.
61	Map	ACL, modified.
61	Map	ACL, modified.
61	Image	Courtesy of AIATSIS, Alick Jackomos Collection, item JACKOMOS.A03.BW-N3795_04.
62	Image	Reproduced by permission of Brenda Gifford.
62	Map	ABS.
63	Image	Howard Morphy.
63	Image	Maggie Brady.
63	Image	Reproduced by permission of Cairns Regional Gallery.
64	Image	Chauvel Film Enterprises.
65	Image	Courtesy of Barefoot Communications.

Page	**Chapter 13** Art	
67	Image	Alan Thorne.
67	Image	Courtesy of AIATSIS, Howard P. McNickle Collection, item MCNICKLE.H03.CS-83224; and Cairns & Harney 2003, p. 83.
67	Map	ACL.
67	Image	Bill Arthur.
68	Image	Reproduced by permission of Wunambal Gaambera Aboriginal Corporation.
68	Image	Courtesy of Dr Paul S.C.Taçon.
69	Image	Howard Morphy.
69	Image	Reproduced by permission of Wunambal Gaambera Aboriginal Corporation.
70	Map	ACL.
70	Image	Courtesy of AIATSIS, Tamsin Donaldson Collection, item DONALDSON.T13.BW-N4396. Photograph by Dr Tamsin Donaldson. Reproduced by permission of the Orange Local Aboriginal Land Council.
71	Map	ABS.
71	Image	Kluge-Ruhe Aboriginal Art Collection, University of Virginia. © estate of the artist licensed by Aboriginal Artists Agency Ltd.
72	Image	Kluge-Ruhe Aboriginal Art Collection, University of Virginia. © Nancy Nanimurra/Copyright Agency, 2021.
72	Image	Kluge-Ruhe Aboriginal Art Collection, University of Virginia. Reproduced by permission of Injalak Arts and Crafts, Gunbalanya, Northern Territory. © Lofty Bardayal Nadjamerrek/Copyright Agency, 2021.
73	Image	National Gallery of Australia, Canberra (where it is titled Rover Thomas [Joolama], Kalumpiwarra 1984). © Rover Thomas/Copyright Agency, 2021.
73	Image	Dundiwuy Wanambi, *Spirit figure with wallaby* 1987. Beach hibiscus, ochres, PVA, bark. 171.5 cm. State Art Collection, Art Gallery of Western Australia. Purchased 1987. Reproduced by permission of Buku-Larrnggay Mulka Centre.
74	Image	Photographer Lynnette Griffiths. Reproduced by permission of Erub Arts.
74	Image	Purchased 1995 Australia Council Funds, 12th National Aboriginal and Torres Strait Islander Art Awards. Museum & Art Gallery of the Northern Territory Collection. ABETH 3344. Reproduced by permission of Hermannsburg Potters.

Page	**Chapter 14** Sports	
75	Image	Courtesy of AIATSIS, Aldo Massola Collection, item MASSOLA.A01.BW-N02395_01.
75	Graph	Macquarie Dictionary Publishers.
76	Map	ABS.
76	Map	ABS.
77	Image	Steven Siewert/Fairfax Syndication. Reproduced with permission by the Lajamanu community.

78	Image	Wayne Ludbey/Fairfax Syndication.
78	Image	David Callow, courtesy of SPORT, The Library.
79	Map	ABS.
79	Image	Courtesy of the Indigenous Marathon Foundation.

Page	**Chapter 15** Games and toys	
80	Image	Courtesy of Australian Museum Archives AM320/v05170. Photographer Frank Hurley. Reproduced by kind permission of Mer Gedkem Le (Torres Strait Islanders) Corporation RNTBC, on behalf of the Meriam People of Mer, Dauar and Waier Islands.
80	Image	Haagen 1994, reproduced with permission of the National Museum of Australia.
81	Image	Courtesy of Australian Museum Archives AMS391/M2687/7. Reproduced by permission of Djiru Warrangburra Aboriginal Corporation RNTBC.
81	Image	Macquarie Dictionary Publishers.
81	Image	Courtesy of AIATSIS, Jon C. Altman Collection, item ALTMAN.J01.CS-69804. Reproduced by permission of Jon Altman and Maningrida Arts Centre.
81	Image	Courtesy of AIATSIS, Ute Eickelkamp Collection, item EICKELKAMP.U01.CS-118343. Reproduced with permission of Ernabella Arts Inc.
82	Image	Reproduced by permission of the Western Desert Verbal Arts Project and artist Joella Butler. This research was primarily supported by ELDP (Endangered Languages Documentation Programme) Small Grant SG0187 and an Australian Research Council-Discovery Indigenous Fellowship for Elizabeth Ellis (IN150100018).
82	Image	Reproduced by permission of Gerald McGregor.

Page	**Chapter 16** Language	
84	Map	This map attempts to represent the language, social or nation groups of Aboriginal Australia. It shows only the general locations of larger groupings of people which may include clans, dialects or individual languages in a group. It used published resources from 1988-1994 and is not intended to be exact, nor the boundaries fixed. It is not suitable for native title or other land claims. David R Horton (creator), © Aboriginal Studies Press, AIATSIS, 1996. No reproduction without permission. To purchase a print version visit: www.aiatsis.ashop.com.au/
85	Map	ACL, modified.
86	Map	ACL.
86	Map	ACL.
87	Map	ABS map from 2016 Census; customised from Australian Statistical Geography 2016, Indigenous Areas.
87	Map	ABS map from 2016 Census; customised from Australian Statistical Geography 2016, Indigenous Areas.
88	Map	ABS.
89	Map	ABS map from 2016 Census; customised from Australian Statistical Geography 2016, Indigenous Areas.

89	Map	ABS map from 2016 Census; customised from Australian Statistical Geography 2016, Indigenous Areas. ABS, modified.
90	Map	ABS map from 2016 Census; customised from Australian Statistical Geography 2016, Indigenous Areas. ABS, modified.
90	Map	ABS map from 2016 Census; customised from Australian Statistical Geography 2016, Indigenous Areas. ABS, modified.
91	Map	ABS.
91	Map	ABS.

Page	**Chapter 17** Placenames	
92	Image	Frances Morphy.
93	Image	Harold Koch.
93	Graph	Macquarie Dictionary Publishers.
93	Image	Harold Koch.
94	Map	ACL, modified.
94	Map	ACL, modified.
95	Image	John Coppi, CSIRO.
96	Map	ACL, modified.

Page	**Chapter 18** Land and water	
97	Map	ACL.
97	Map	ACL.
98	Map	ACL.
99	Image	Frances Morphy.
99	Image	Australian National Maritime Museum Saltwater Collection. Reproduced courtesy of the artist, Gawirrin Gumana 1935–2016, museum and Buku-Larrnggay Mulka Centre.
100	Map	ABS, modified.
101	Map	ABS, modified.
101	Map	ABS, modified.

Page	**Chapter 19** Environment and Country	
102	Map	ACL.
103	Map	ABS.
104	Image	Elizabeth McCrudden. Supplied by the Centre for Invasive Species Solutions.
104	Map	Based on Williams, J. et al. *Australia state of the environment report 2001 (theme report)*, CSIRO Publishing on behalf of the Department of the Environment and Heritage, Canberra. ABS, modified.

105	Map	Based on Symonds, J. L. 1985, *A history of British atomic tests in Australia*, Australian Government Publishing Service, and Morton S. et al. 2013, *Art, Science and Stories from Paraku*, CSIRO Publishing. © Commonwealth of Australia reproduced by permission. ACL.
105	Image	Brad Fleet/Newspix.
106	Map	ABS.
106	Image	Donna Green.
107	Image	Donna Green.
108	Map	ABS, modified.
109	Map	ABS.
109	Image	Glenn Campbell/Fairfax Syndication.

Page	**Chapter 20** Colonialism and violence	
110	Map	ACL.
110	Map	ACL.
110	Map	ACL.
111	Map	ACL.
111	Map	ACL.
111	Map	ACL.
112	Map	ACL, modified.
112	Map	ABS, modified.
112	Map	ACL, modified.
113	Map	ACL.
114	Map	ACL, modified.
115	Image	Dragi Markovic, National Museum of Australia. NMA Object 7287.
115	Map	ACL.
116	Map	ABS 2016 remote areas map.

Page	**Chapter 21** Social justice	
117	Map	ABS map from the 2015 National Aboriginal and Torres Strait Islander Social Survey; customised from Australian Statistical Geography 2011, Indigenous Regions.
118	Map	ACL, modified.
118	Image	© Brenda L. Croft/Copyright Agency, 2021.
119	Speech	Commonwealth of Australia.
120	Image	Louise Whelan, Canberra, 13 February 2008. National Library of Australia, PIC/12270/7.
121	Graph	Macquarie Dictionary Publishers.
121	Map	ABS map from the 2015 National Aboriginal and Torres Strait Islander Social Survey; customised from Australian Statistical Geography 2011, Indigenous Regions.

Page	**Chapter 22** Protest	
122	Map	ACL, modified.
123	Image	Purchased 1990, 7th National Aboriginal and Torres Strait Islander Art Awards. Museum & Art Gallery of the Northern Territory Collection. ABART 1060, purchased from the 7th National Aboriginal Art Award. Reproduced courtesy of the artist's estate and Roslyn Oxley9 Gallery, Sydney.
123	Image	Neville Whitemarsh, Newspix. Reproduced by permission of the Perkins family.
124	Map	ACL, modified.
125	Image	Courtesy of the artist Daniel Boyd.
125	Image	Mick Tsikas/AAP.

Page	**Chapter 23** Symbols of nationhood	
126	Image	Mick Tsikas/AAP.
126	Image	Reproduced by permission of Island Co-ordinating Council. Flag designer: the late Bernard Namok.
126	Image	Fairfax Syndication.
127	Image	Will Sanders.
128	Image	Photographer Amy Johannes, Melbourne Law School.
129	Image	Thomas Mayor. Photograph taken at Gurindji Freedom Day 2017.

Page	**Chapter 24** Population and residence	
130	Graph	Macquarie Dictionary Publishers.
131	Map	ABS 2003; ABS 2016 remote areas map.
131	Map	ABS map from 2016 Census; customised from Australian Statistical Geography 2016, Indigenous Areas.
132	Map	ABS map from 2016 Census; customised from Australian Statistical Geography 2016, Indigenous Areas.
133	Map	ABS 2006 Community Housing and Infrastructure Needs Survey.
134	Image	Will Sanders.
134	Image	Courtesy of AIATSIS, La Perouse Collection, item LAPEROUSE.001.CS-S00261_20.

Page	**Chapter 25** Education	
135	Image	Ian Dunlop. Reproduced with permission by Narritjin's family.
135	Image	Approval given by CAYLUS and the Utopia School.
136	Image	Bill Arthur.
136	Map	ABS.
137	Map	ABS map from 2016 Census; customised from Australian Statistical Geography 2016, Indigenous Areas.

137	Map	ABS map from 2016 Census; customised from Australian Statistical Geography 2016, Indigenous Areas.
138	Image	Reproduced by permission of the Perkins family.
138	Map	ABS map from 2016 Census; customised from Australian Statistical Geography 2016, Indigenous Areas.

Page	**Chapter 26** Working life	
139	Map	ABS map from 2016 Census; customised from Australian Statistical Geography 2016, Indigenous Areas.
140	Map	ABS map from 2016 Census; customised from Australian Statistical Geography 2016, Indigenous Areas.
140	Image	National Archives of Australia A1200, L13068.
141	Map	ABS map from 2016 Census; customised from Australian Statistical Geography 2016, Indigenous Areas.
141	Map	ABS map from 2016 Census; customised from Australian Statistical Geography 2016, Indigenous Areas.
142	Map	ABS map from 2016 Census; customised from Australian Statistical Geography 2016, Indigenous Areas.
143	Map	ABS map from the 2015 National Aboriginal and Torres Strait Islander Social Survey; to the 2011 Australian Statistical Geography, Indigenous Regions.
143	Image	Courtesy of AIATSIS, Moonbird Collection, item MOONBIRD.001.BW-B00765_09.
144	Image	Reproduced by permission of Julian Gorman and Tony Griffiths, Charles Darwin University.
144	Image	Courtesy of AIATSIS, Jon C. Altman Collection, item ALTMAN.J01.BW-N3217_14. Reproduced by permission of Jon Altman and Maningrida Arts Centre.
144	Image	Courtesy of AIATSIS, Jon C. Altman Collection, item ALTMAN.J01.BW-N3215_03. Reproduced by permission of Jon Altman and Maningrida Arts Centre.

Page	**Chapter 27** Health and wellbeing	
145	Map	ACL, modified.
146	Map	ACL, modified.
146	Map	ACL, modified.
147	Map	ACL, modified.
147	Map	ACL.
147	Image	Macquarie Dictionary Publishers.
148	Image	Courtesy of AIATSIS, TWEEDIE.P1.CS-64784. Reproduced by permission of Maningrida Arts Centre.
148	Map	ACL, modified.
149	Image	Pregnancy, Artist Marie McMahan/Redback Graphix.
149	Image	NPY Women's Council.

Index

Cover artwork

Kungkarrangkalpa Tjurkurpa, 2015, is a collaborative painting made by Anawari Inpiti Mitchell, Angilyiya Tjapitji Mitchell, Lalla West, Jennifer Nginyaka Mitchell, Eileen Tjayanka Woods, Lesley Laidlaw and Robert Woods.

The Seven Sisters Songline refers to the Pleiades constellation. It travels from the west to the east across the far western and central deserts. The sisters are pursued by a man, Yurla in the west and Wati Nyiru further east, who is a shapeshifter with transformative powers. He becomes particularly besotted with one of the sisters and pursues them endlessly in order to possess them. Today, this saga is visible in the Orion constellation and the Pleiades star cluster as a constant reminder of the consequences of attempting to possess something through wrongful means.

Environment and deep history from 70 000

	70 000–60 000 BEFORE PRESENT	60 000–50 000 BEFORE PRESENT	50 000–40 000 BEFORE PRESENT	40 000–30 000 BEFORE PRESENT	30 000–20 000 BEFORE PRESENT
SEA LEVEL	Sea level 75m lower than present Australia and PNG connected	Sea level 50m lower than present	Sea level 50–55m lower than present	Sea level 60m lower than present	Sea level starts dropping Sea level reaches 130m lower than present
ENVIRONMENT			A wetter period begins Willandra Lakes around Lake Mungo, Lake Bass, and Lake Carpentaria are all formed Some megafauna become extinct		Start of last glacial period Drier conditions begin Temperature drops Large marsupials become extinct
OCCUPATION	First people arrive from South-East Asia	People are living in Arnhem Land, NT and south-west NSW		Central Australia and Tasmania are occupied	Archaeological sites are over much of the continent People leave parts of central deserts
CULTURAL FEATURES	World's first oceanic crossing, from South-East Asia World's earliest edge-ground axe-heads in Arnhem Land, NT	Ochre at archaeological sites, Arnhem Land, NT	World's earliest cremation burial and burial with ochre, Lake Mungo, NSW Earliest evidence of rock paintings and engravings, WA	Ochre mine at Karrku near Yuendumu, NT Edge ground stone tools, Qld Shell necklace, north-west WA	Large ochre quarries Bone tools made, south-west WA Grinding stones used near Brewarrina, NSW Finger markings in Koonalda Cave, SA

YEARS OF OCCUPATION

INDIGENOUS Approximately 70 000 years ago to present

INDIGENOUS and NON-INDIGENOUS 1788 to the present